LEARNING TO LISTEN:

A STRATEGY-BASED APPROACH
FOR THE SECOND-LANGUAGE LEARNER

D1476176

DAVID J. MENDELSOHN, PH. D.

DOMINIE PRESS, INC.

Publisher: Raymond Yuen

Project Editor: Dan Edelman

Text Designer: Becky Colgan

Cover Designer: Gary Hamada

Published by:

🔏 **Dominie Press, Inc.**

1949 Kellogg Avenue
Carlsbad, CA 92008 USA

ISBN 1-56270-299-8

Printed in U.S.A.

2 3 4 5 6 7 8 9 C 03 02 01 00

www.dominie.com

Dedication

This book is dedicated to my wonderful, loving, and supportive family—my wife, Jenny, and my children, Lee, Noa, and Jonathan.

Contents

Acknowledgments

First I would like to thank my friends and colleagues, Maureen McNerney and Hitay Yukseker, who read and provided feedback on earlier manuscripts out of which this book has grown.

I owe a particularly large debt of gratitude to two more friends and colleagues: Rena Helms-Park, who tirelessly and uncomplainingly read and commented on each chapter as it was completed; and Michael Rost, whose review of the full manuscript was invaluable!

Thanks are also due to Gillian Brown, my professor and mentor of many years ago, whose inspiration and academic rigor have served as an example and a model for me ever since.

Finally, I would like to thank Raymond Yuen, Chief Executive Officer of Dominie Press, for his support and for the faith that he has had in me over many years of collaboration. It is indeed a pleasure and a privilege to publish with a person of such high integrity as Raymond.

PREFACE

Learning to Listen: A Strategy-Based Approach for the Second-Language Learner deals with the teaching of listening comprehension to second-language speakers. The strategy-based approach that is described and exemplified is applicable at all levels of listening proficiency.

Learning to Listen advocates training students to consciously work with strategies that help in comprehension. The "strategy-based" approach trains students *how to listen*—how to use linguistic, paralinguistic, and extralinguistic signals to best predict, make inferences, and hypothesize total meaning.

Learning to Listen is a book for practicing ESL/EFL teachers, and teachers-in-training. In the book I argue that the more conventional ways of handling listening comprehension are not the most efficient, and suggest that by applying recent research on learning strategies, teachers should become strategy trainers, training their students to listen by using strategies to get at meaning.

Chapters 1 and 2 discuss the theoretical assumptions concerning the learning process in general, the listening process, and learning and listening strategies, on which the strategy-based approach is based. Chapter 3 then argues the case for a strategy-based approach.

Chapter 4 discusses the essential features and design of a strategy-based listening course, while Chapter 5 is devoted to the linguistic proficiency required in order to be a competent listener.

Chapters 6–9 exemplify the strategy-based approach, showing sample activities and how they train students to use strategies of different kinds to get at meaning. This classroom approach derives from the notion that any good second-language pedagogy involves training students "how to do something" (in this case, how to listen). This, in turn, involves training in the application of different strategies. This strategy training is aimed at the learner ultimately achieving greater learner autonomy. Each of these chapters addresses a different aspect of teaching listening comprehension. The intent is to provide concrete ideas and suggestions to teachers and teachers-in-training as to how to teach listening comprehension.

Finally, Chapter 10 discusses how it is necessary to both bring all the training together at the end of a listening course and to provide a lot of practice.

1

Learning and Listening:
Theoretical Assumptions

1.1 Introductory Comments

Listening plays a very important part in second-language acquisition, to the point that certain methodologies have been built on this fact. Two examples are Asher's "Total Physical Response" (1969) and Krashen and Terrell's "Natural Approach" (1983).

In addition, of the total time spent on communicating, listening takes up 40–50%; speaking, 25–30%; reading, 11–16%; and writing, about 9% (Rivers 1981; Oxford 1993). What is more, a survey done by Yorio (1982) of 454 students in an intensive ESL program showed that the *students themselves* clearly recognized the importance of listening, and expressed the desire that more of it be taught.

Listening comprehension is so important because when listening, listeners often have no control over what will be "coming at" them, particularly in one-way communication situations, as in a lecture. Listeners have no control over what is going to be said, how it is going to be said, and how quickly it is going to be said. In two-way communication, as in dialogue, the listener's responses and reactions do influence the speaker. The situation is quite different with speaking, where the speaker can get meaning across with limited proficiency by judicious use of communication strategies. Even with reading, there is not the same time pressure, and readers can both go back over what they have read, and resort to a dictionary if they wish to. In listening, the transient spoken word "comes at" listeners very fast and is gone!

And yet, despite a gradually increasing acceptance of the importance of listening comprehension for second-language learners, the teaching of listening comprehension remains a somewhat neglected and poorly taught aspect of English in many ESL programs—the "Cinderella" skill of ESL.

There are three main reasons for neglected or poorly taught listening. The first is that until a few decades ago, it was not broadly accepted that listening comprehension *should* be taught explicitly. The argument supporting this is what I cynically call the "osmosis" approach (Mendelsohn 1984): students are listening to the teacher all day in any case, and will therefore improve their listening comprehension through this. Furthermore, the focus on production in the audiolingual method is partly to blame for this situation. (For a survey of the past twenty-five years of teaching listening comprehension, see Gillian Brown, 1987.)

The second reason for poorly taught listening comprehension is that average classroom teachers do not feel confident teaching listening, and in fact have not taught their students "how to" go about it, but have, at best, provided a lot of listening practice. This is an improvement on the "osmosis" approach, but still mainly provides only exposure to listening, without teaching students what to do.

The tasks assigned were also often inappropriate. The problem is partly teacher-induced. In order to change this, it is necessary that ESL teachers develop an even greater commitment to the teaching of listening comprehension. However, this will only happen when teachers not only have a greater understanding of the makeup of the spoken language and the complexity of the listening process, but also have available to them methodologies proven to be beneficial to their students.[1]

The third reason why listening comprehension has often been poorly taught is that traditional listening comprehension materials for second-language learners are often unsuitable for teaching listening comprehension. I examined eighteen ESL listening comprehension courses published between 1972 and 1988 (thirteen published in the U.S. and five published in Britain), and found only two (one published in 1986, and one in 1988) to be really impressive:

i.   Only two of the eighteen (11%) teach the students *how to listen*—an essential feature of my approach. Coupled with this, many of the tasks and activities required students to listen in a way they would never listen in the real world. For example, students listened to a social "chat" but were then asked questions on minute details. As will be discussed below, this leads to bad listening habits!

ii. The material listened to in more than half of the courses is not representative of the spoken English of the real world. Either it is written language that has been read out loud and recorded, or it is a clearly scripted simulation of spoken language, which sounds stilted and artificial. (It must, however, be noted that both in the recent literature about teaching listening and in the courses themselves, an effort is being made to make the material authentic. Ironically, sev-

---

[1] While it is true that listening comprehension has traditionally been very poorly taught, there are a number of books on listening and the listening process that have made major contributions to improving the situation, notably those by Gillian Brown (1977, 1990); Ur (1984); Anderson and Lynch (1988); and Rost (1990).

eral of the courses that I criticize on this point claim "authenticity," but I would strongly disagree.)

iii. The approach and criteria for choice of course materials seems in several cases to have been rather haphazard; there was no clear-cut system or sound pedagogical reason for the inclusion of the passages that were chosen. Several of the courses were "situation-based"; the author took care to ensure that, for example, there would be passages from different situations or settings which the learners would probably find themselves in: *At the doctor's office; In the supermarket; At the job interview; In the bank*, etc. Two of the courses' content were grammatically based, one published as recently as 1984! This approach, I believe, relegates listening to an exemplification of a particular structure, rather than focusing on comprehension.

My "strategy-based approach" offers an alternative way to organize a listening comprehension course. Furthermore, drawing on the learning strategy literature, it offers a way of teaching students how to tackle their listening by means of strategies, thereby making them better and more autonomous listeners.

1.2. Some Assumptions About Learning Directly Applicable to a Strategy-Based Approach to Teaching Listening

Jones, Palincsar, Ogle, and Carr (1987), in their excellent book *Strategic Teaching and Learning*, describe a series of "research-based" statements about learning, which provide strong support for a "strategy-based" approach for listening comprehension:

i. The skilled learner strives to achieve two goals: "to understand the meaning of the tasks at hand [in our case, to comprehend what is being listened to], and to regulate his or her own learning [in our case to become an autonomous learner]" (p.4).

ii. Learning is characterized as "thinking, that is, as using prior knowledge and specific strategies to understand the ideas in a text as a whole or the elements of a problem as a whole" (p.5).

iii. "Learning is strategic" (p.14), and Jones et al. use this as the basis for their "strategic teaching" approach, and for strategy training, which they strongly endorse throughout their book.

iv. Learning occurs in three phases: preparing for learning (in our case, prelistening), on-line processing (in our case, the listening itself), and consolidating/extending, which is connected to what they call "anticipating." (In terms of listening comprehension, this concept relates to predicting, guessing, and inferencing.)

v. Students can be taught to use various strategies, and Jones, Palincsar, Ogle, and Carr cite research evidence on low- achieving students to support this.

1.3. Schema Theory

Rumelhart (1980:34), building on the early work of Bartlett (1932), provides an excellent explanation of schema theory and its place in cognition:

> A schema theory is basically a theory about knowledge. It is a theory about how knowledge is represented and about how that representation facilitates the use of the knowledge in particular ways. According to schema theories, all knowledge is packaged into units. These units are the schemata.

He goes on to explain that "a schema theory embodies a prototype theory of meaning," i.e., the meaning of that concept in normal situations. He draws the analogy between a schema and the script of a play, pointing out that different actors may play a character differently, but this does not change the essential nature of the play. "So a schema has *variables* that can be associated with (bound to) different aspects of the environment on different instantiations of the schema" (p.35). The schema allows for variation and merely serves as a "skeleton around which the situation is interpreted" (Rumelhart 1980:37). Schank and Abelson (1977:41) define schemata (scripts) as "predetermined stereotyped sequences of actions that define well-known situations."

Chiang and Dunkel (1992:350) explain the significance of schema theory for listening comprehension and interpretation (which I discuss below) as follows:

> The basic tenet of schema theory posits that written text, or spoken discourse, does not carry meaning in and of itself. Rather, meaning occurs as a result of the interaction between the reader's or listener's prior knowledge about the world and the text or speech.

Activating a schema, a package of prior knowledge, also makes hypothesis formation, predicting, and inferencing possible. As will be discussed below, these are essential processes for listening.

Schemata are of two types: content schemata and rhetorical schemata.

Content schemata are networks of knowledge on different topics that an individual has stored in the brain, and are able to be activated in various ways (Rumelhart, Smolensky, McClelland, and Hinton 1986). For example, knowing that the topic is "terrorism" or that the location at which something is said is "at the box office," activates the individual's knowledge on the topic, and results in certain expectations being set up. It should be noted that one of the difficulties for second-language speakers is that they may lack the schema in question, for example for "the World Series." Perhaps even more problematic is when they have a schema for, say, "funerals," but are unaware that it is not the same as the schema that this term activates in other cultures.

Rhetorical schemata (also known as "organizational" or "textual" schemata) relate to a knowledge of the structure and organization of the discourse. An awareness that what is being listened to is, for example, a job interview or a recipe will set up certain expectations as to the format and organization of these types of discourse.

The literature, albeit often related to reading comprehension, is replete with claims for the importance of both types of schemata and the importance of background knowledge (Carrell 1984; Weissenreider 1987; Long 1989 [deals directly with listening]; Chiang and Dunkel 1992).

An acceptance of the notion of schema and the way knowledge is stored in units in the brain, is very important in understanding the theoretical underpinnings of my strategy-based approach to listening comprehension. As is reiterated throughout the book, many of the strategies I recommend for getting at the meaning of a listening passage, and particularly prelistening and drawing on prior knowledge, are predicated on the notion of activating existing schemata in the minds of listeners. Activation of these schemata facilitates the making of predictions and inferences (Anderson, Reynolds, Schallert, and Goetz 1977; Clarke and Silberstein 1977). It should be noted that much of the seminal work in this area was done in relation to reading rather than to listening, but it certainly holds true for listening too.

The way in which schema theory connects with the vital listening strategy of inferencing is explained by Rumelhart using the example of a schema about "buying." As he explains: "If we take a certain transaction to be one of BUYING but do not notice the MONEY, we can *infer* that there was MONEY and that, in fact, the MONEY probably was money amounting in value to about the value of the MERCHANDISE. In this way, the schema can help us make inferences about unobserved aspects of a situation" (p.36). It is the activation of the schema that makes these inferences and assumptions possible. Carrell and Eisterhold (1983:559) make this even clearer when they state that "much of the meaning understood from a text is really not actually in the text, per se, but in the reader, in the background or schematic knowledge of the reader."

While acknowledging the value of activating schemata for processing listening, there is also a danger that must be noted: the activation of a schema early on in a listening passage may "strait-jacket" the mind of listeners, causing them to stick with an incorrect hypothesis and therefore an incorrect understanding of the whole text. What is more, as Long (1989:33) points out, they "work well for routine events, but tend to break down in novel contexts." It is for this reason that I advocate training learners to go through the "hypothesis-formation/hypothesis-modification" process (see Chapter 8), so that they should become accepting of the fact that often their initial hypothesis will be incorrect, and will require significant modification.

1.4. Some Essential Features of the Listening Process

1.4.1. Listening Is an Interpretive Process

One of the things that has detrimentally affected attitudes to listening comprehension in ESL courses in the past is that listening has been treated as if it were an activity in which competent listeners comprehend *precisely* what the speaker intended to communicate. The goal was seen as decoding the message, yielding *the* text. This is ironic since it has been accepted for the longest time that *reading* is an interpretive process. Few English teachers today would argue otherwise. Listening, like reading, is an interpretive process. Murphy (1985:23), citing his doctoral research, characterizes the interpretive nature of listening as follows: "Listeners generate internal texts which commonly differ from what they hear in unexpected ways." An acceptance of listening as being interpretive impacts on the notion of "correctness" in a listening comprehension course. Gillian Brown (1987:14) takes this notion a step further and talks of the "imaginative effort" involved in communicating, and goes on to point out that an acceptance of this view of listening makes context crucial to meaning.[2]

1.4.2. Listening Is an Active Process

Traditionally, listening has been seen by ESL teachers as a passive activity; listeners passively receive the message sent by speakers. Not only is listening an interpretive process, but I see it as an activity in which learners are *active—* fully as active as when speaking. This leads to the notion that our mandate as teachers of listening is to train our students how to be the most efficient and active listeners possible through the use of a series of strategies. Hence, I have called my approach a strategy-based approach to the teaching of listening comprehension.

1.4.3. Listening Is Often Interactive

In the real world, we seldom listen to extended monologue outside of academic or quasi-academic settings. Not only is the bulk of what we listen to dialogue, but we are very often active participants in the interaction. This therefore implies that listening and speaking are very often intertwined, a point which should be borne in mind when designing listening comprehension courses. Not only does interactional listening require training and practice, but learners doing such listening have to be trained and encouraged to use the social strategy of asking for clarification from their interlocutors.

1.4.4. Listening Can Be Approached "Bottom-Up" or "Top-Down"

Bottom-up processing involves piecing together, in a linear fashion, the parts of what is being heard, so that ultimately the whole content will be clear.

---

[2] See also Sperber and Wilson 1986; Rost 1990.

It is like joining together the links in a chain, one by one, in sequence.

Top-down processing, which I am advocating, is holistic. It goes "from whole to part" (Rumelhart 1980:41). It is built on the premise that listening is an interpretive process. Listeners should be actively formulating a hypothesis very early on in the listening. This hypothesis ("model") should be based on what is heard, and linked to the listeners' background knowledge (schemata). Then, as the listening continues, listeners should be modifying or verifying their hypothesis.

Anderson and Lynch (1988:9, 11) capture the difference between these processes very clearly by describing bottom-up processing as the following: "listener as tape recorder," and top-down processing as "listener as active model builder."

Listening should, on the whole, be approached top-down because of the vast amount of interpretive work that listeners do, in addition to trying to link what they are listening to with their prior knowledge. However, this does not mean that there is no place at all for bottom-up procedures or strategies. The top-down approach, which is the one that native speakers use, is not available to beginner ESL listeners. Consequently, they have to do some bottom-up processing of what they hear at the acoustic level to facilitate subsequent top-down processing (Byrnes 1984; Gillian Brown 1990).

As will become evident in the subsequent chapters, the strategy-based approach that I am advocating makes maximum use of a top-down approach where feasible, but also uses bottom-up strategies where they are deemed useful to learners. For example, prelistening and stressing the importance of hypothesizing, and predicting and guessing, are instances of top-down strategies, while listening for key transitions in a discourse is a bottom-up strategy.

Further justification for the presence of strategies from both categories in a listening course is that different approaches fit the different learning styles of different learners: those who tend to concentrate on fluency rather than accuracy will be most comfortable with the top-down strategies, while those who value accuracy very highly will prefer the bottom-up strategies. In addition, top-down and bottom-up strategies can compensate for each other: "For example, proficient listeners use their knowledge of lexis and topic to interpret the confusing sounds in the speech stream. . . . On the other hand, they also use their basic decoding skills to check the progress of the argument" (Peterson 1991:110).

Native speakers approach most listening top-down, and I will argue that what we should be doing in an ESL listening course is "unlocking" for listeners their first-language listening strategies when listening in the second language.[3]

---

[3] For a comprehensive list of activities classified according to whether they are "bottom-up" or "top-down," see Richards (1990:59-62).

1.5. Some Essential Features of Spoken English

1.5.1. There Are Substantial Differences Between Spoken and Written Language

When planning a listening comprehension course, it is very important that the course reflects the fact that spoken English varies in significant ways from written language, not only in form but also in purpose. A major proportion of spoken discourse is not for the purpose of imparting or communicating important facts or information, but rather to be friendly or to "chat." Small talk is an obvious example of this, in which speech is a form of social interaction. Also, as Tannen (1982:41) points out, unlike written discourse, spoken discourse "establishes cohesion through paralinguistic features [not through lexicalization]"—hence the importance of paralinguistics in a listening course. These differences are sufficiently large that second-language learners need to be made aware of them, and the listening materials must be spoken English, and not an oral rendition of what is essentially written English.

However, as Tannen (1982) very clearly points out, the distinction between spoken and written language ("orality" and "literacy") is not an absolute split. Clearly, there are features usually associated with written language that are present in certain forms of spoken discourse. For example, focusing on content, which is usually associated with written discourse, is also a major distinguishing feature of spoken *academic* discourse. However, for most spoken discourse, this spoken/written distinction is a useful one.

The following are some of the most significant differences:

i.   Spoken language often occurs for a very different purpose than written language. Its purpose is often social interaction and the maintenance of social relations. Conversely, in the majority of written English texts, conveying the cognitive content is most important. This is a major difference, and one that should impact on the planning of a good listening comprehension course. What is more, even when information is being transmitted in the spoken mode, the amount of cognitive content, i.e., the amount of information being transmitted in any measured unit of language, is lower in spoken than in written English. This is caused by two major factors: the increased redundancy and the presence of "empty verbal fillers" in spoken English.

Genuine spoken language is rich in redundancy—in repetition, restatement, redefinition, and paraphrase; and there are teachable discourse markers that signal many of these, such as "in other words" or "by that I mean." This redundancy provides the listeners with additional chances to pick up anything they might have missed—something that second-language learners should be trained to take maximum advantage of.

Coupled with the inherent redundancy is the presence of "fillers" which are often real English words such as "you see" or "the truth of the matter is." These fillers, which contribute virtually nothing to the cognitive content of what is being said, serve the purpose of permitting the speakers to gather their thoughts without being in danger of losing the floor.

ii.   The syntax used in spoken English is somewhat different than in written English: it is often simpler, and it is often less "correct," by prescriptive standards. Written English contains more embedding and more subordination than spoken English. For example, there is very little use of nondefining relative clauses in spoken English. We are unlikely to hear such utterances as, "Elvis Presley, who was an extremely famous rock star, had a southern accent," and are more likely to hear something like, "Elvis Presley had a southern accent. He was an extremely famous rock star." Complex sentences with embeddings require more mental processing, and are not very frequent in spoken discourse. Moreover, we are quite likely to hear utterances, even in the spoken English of educated native speakers, that would not be considered grammatically acceptable or complete if they appeared in written form. This is often a result of the speaker losing the thread. For example, it would not be unusual for a speaker to say something like the following, and for it to go uncorrected: "Apples and oranges imported from a country that has a warmer climate is better."

iii. Not only is the syntax of spoken English often "less correct," but the organization of what is being said is often "poor" by written English standards. Not having the text in front of them or the time to monitor carefully, speakers of English often produce poorly organized and repetitive spoken discourse. There are even instances in which a speaker says the opposite of what was intended.

iv.   The spoken language is far richer in prosodic features than the written language. When speaking, it is possible to use such features as speed of delivery, loudness, and softness; facial and body gesture; changes in intonation; and much more, while in written language all that we have is a very limited punctuation system. This difference works to the advantage of the second-language listeners, provided that they are trained to utilize these features.

v.   Rapid spoken English ("fast speech") has its own pronunciation rules, and real spoken language is not merely a stringing together of words pronounced the way they are represented in a dictionary in "citation" form. There are a number of "fast-speech" rules which make listening to spoken English quite difficult for second-language learners, particularly if they have not been exposed to these features (see Chapter 5).

vi.   Spoken language will often occur in dialogue, often with the listener being an active participant, thereby requiring participants to monitor their interlocutors' reactions and modify their responses accordingly.

vii. Real, spontaneous spoken English, on the whole, tends to be less formal than written English. This is reflected at all levels of the language. For example, there is a much greater use of short forms such as, "He's finished," together with much more colloquial register. Unfortunately, this is not reflected in many traditional ESL listening comprehension materials. They tend to be unrealistically formal, thereby exposing learners to a style that they are less likely to encounter in reality.

viii. Paralinguistic features are extremely important in spoken discourse. In fact, as Tannen (1982:41) points out, "In speaking, everything that is said must be said in some way: at some pitch, in some tone of voice. . . . All these nonverbal and paralinguistic features reveal the speaker's attitude . . . and establish cohesion."

1.5.2. Spoken English Has Several Forms

Spoken English does not occur in one single form. There are several different types of spoken English, and our learners have to be trained to handle most of them. Some of these are interactional in function and display the features of spoken discourse, while others are not interactional (transactional) and, in fact, display features usually associated with written discourse. Examples of different types of spoken language are the following: spontaneous spoken language (e.g., a chat between friends, a conversation between colleagues); spontaneous, but careful spoken language, often drawing on some notes (e.g., a response to a question at the end of a lecture); very careful and deliberate spoken language usually controlled through the use of notes (e.g., a public lecture); and spoken language that is in fact a reading of something written (e.g., radio news).[4]

Ur (1984:2) provides an extensive list of examples of the different types of listening that people do in real life. These lists and categorizations can be refined ad infinitum, and, in addition, we could add such variables as variations in genre—each with its specific discourse features (lecture, anecdote, etc.), topic, number of participants, and more. But the important point is that there be a realization of the existence of such differences (see Chapter 9).

---

[4] For a detailed categorization, see Gregory (1967).

1.6. A Definition of Listening Comprehension

The literature abounds in definitions of listening comprehension for second-language speakers and the abilities necessary to be competent listeners. I define listening comprehension as "the ability to understand the spoken language of native speakers" (Mendelsohn 1984:64). This is a useful "one-line definition" serving as a starting point. Moreover, my definition, with its clear communicative objective, stands in stark contrast to the way in which listening was addressed in the audiolingual paradigm: "A student 'listens' not so much to comprehend as to mimic (in repetition drill) or to respond in correct form (in pattern response drill)" (Nord 1980:5–6). I would argue that listening in the audiolingual programs has little to do with real listening *comprehension* and how to teach it.

O'Malley, Chamot, and Kupper (1989:434) offer a useful, and much more extensive definition:

> Listening comprehension is an active and conscious process in which the listener constructs meaning by using cues from contextual information and from existing knowledge, while relying upon multiple strategic resources to fulfill the task requirements.

To this definition, it would be wise to add what Byrnes (1984:319) calls "schemd-based understanding," i.e., "information stored in long-term memory as frames or scripts which directs the comprehension process."

1.7. The Abilities Required of a Competent Listener

1.7.1. The Ability to Process the Linguistic Forms

This requires that listeners be able, first and foremost, to *hear* and *distinguish*, from what at first might seem no more than an acoustic blur, the different elements of the linguistic system carrying meaning in the language (discussed in detail in Chapter 5). For example, they must be able to identify that there is a difference between the sounds [e] and [a] as in the words "men" and "man"; that there is a difference between "It's raining" said with a fall in pitch on "raining" (a simple statement of fact), and "It's raining" said with a rise in pitch beginning on "rain-" (an expression of disbelief); that there is a difference between "Jack didn't go," said with the primary sentence stress on "go" (a simple statement of fact), and "Jack didn't go," said with the primary sentence stress on "Jack" (contrastive stress, and paraphrased as "It was Jack and not anyone else you may have been thinking of, who did not go"). What is more, learners must be able to process rapid speech strings like "a bit of a pity" (which sounds something like "@bid@v@piddy," where [@] represents a schwa). The same holds true for the syntactic distinctions in the language. For example, learners have to be able to process elliptical utterances like, "Yes I have," spoken in response to the question "Have you added the chili powder yet?" In addition, to be a competent listener, it is necessary to be able to understand the discourse markers in the spoken language, i.e., signals that speakers provide as to what the relationship between two utterances is, for example, "In contrast . . . " In addition, competent listeners must be able to identify the "meaningless fillers" such as "you see," which give the speaker time to think and competent listeners time to rest, but which can totally throw less-competent listeners.

1.7.2. The Ability to Decipher the Intention of the Speaker

Distinguishing the differences is insufficient. Listeners must also know how to *process* and how to judge what the illocutionary force of an utterance is. That is, what this string of sounds is intended to mean in a particular setting, under a particular set of circumstances—as an act of real communication. For example, they must be able to process "My leg is very painful" in different ways. It could be a simple statement of fact, such as in response to the question "How are you doing"; it could be a refusal to do something, in response to "Would you help me with this suitcase"; or it could be a request for help if the injured person said this while carrying the suitcase.

1.7.3. The Ability to Cope with Listening in an Interaction

As has been stated, much listening is dialogue, and very often listeners are also participants. This then requires competent listeners to be able to listen, process, and, where appropriate, respond almost concurrently. Inability to respond because of being too busy processing what has been said, is inadequate, and I would not call such people competent listeners.

1.7.4. The Ability to Understand the *Whole* Message

Competent listeners must be able not only to comprehend the individual utterances, but also the whole message contained in the discourse. As will be seen in the following example, the meaning of the whole two-utterance discourse is greater than the sum of its parts. First, listeners must be able to comprehend each proposition:

Utterance 1, Proposition 1: The smoke got thicker
and
Utterance 2, Proposition 2: John collapsed

However, without also comprehending that there is a causal relationship between Utterance 1 and Utterance 2, they would not have fully comprehended what was communicated. Note that this also presupposes some world knowledge: thick smoke can cause a person to collapse.

1.7.5. The Ability to Comprehend the Message *Without* Understanding Every Word

Second-language learners often try to listen to and comprehend every word, *word-by-word*. Their subconscious assumption is that this is the way to achieve total comprehension.

When listening in the first language, listeners are able to comprehend much faster speech than we are normally required to listen to (Nichols 1955:300–302). They are able to do this because of *how* they listen, and the fact that they do not listen word-by-word. The problem for second-language learners is that they "fall behind" precisely because of trying to listen word-by-word. They are not using efficient strategies for listening, regardless of how they listen in their first language. Second-language listeners must learn to do what native speakers do when listening. They must be trained to comprehend and interpret the meaning of each utterance and the meaning of the discourse as a whole *without trying to comprehend or hear every word*. We must train them to guess, predict, and inference (see Chapter 8).

1.7.6. The Ability to Recognize Different Genres

Second-language learners have to be familiarized with the different rhetorical genres of the English language. In the spoken language, as in the written language, there are certain "set formats" or "formulas" that different types of English follow. For example, in the academic lecture, there is usually some background introductory material leading to a statement of the lecture's central thesis, followed by clearly "numbered" and identified sections, each supporting the central thesis. Finally, there is usually a "summarizing" conclusion. But even more important than the notion of different genres in larger units of spoken English, is the fact that there are certain formulas within different pieces of spoken discourse. For example, requests and criticisms are usually prefaced by "softeners," and refusals tend not to be stated bluntly: "Much as I would like to help, I just cannot agree to this." Listeners not familiar with these formulas may not process what they are listening to correctly, or will be left behind groping for the importance of the "softeners" and thereby miss the essence of the message.

Second-language learners also need to learn the cultural rules and forms of English. They often have cultural backgrounds that are not similar to English, and therefore are unable to draw on the same world knowledge (also known as "cultural" or "background" knowledge) that native speakers have. In addition, they will not have the "schemata" for different topics ready for activation. These issues of world knowledge and of preexisting schemata are very important features of competent listening.

Learning Strategies and Listening Strategies: Theoretical Assumptions

2.1. A Definition of Learning Strategies

The theoretical basis for my strategy-based approach derives from the literature on learning strategies and its application to the teaching of listening. Chamot (1987:71) provides an excellent basic definition of learning strategies: "Learning strategies are techniques, approaches, or deliberate actions that students take in order to facilitate the learning and recall of both linguistic and content area information."

Willing (1988a:7), in his definition, explicitly states three features of learning strategies that are directly relevant to listening comprehension. He talks of this being a mental procedure for "processing, associating, [and] categorizing" information. All three of these aspects of learning strategies need to be addressed in a listening comprehension course.

Having provided his theoretical definition, Willing goes on to explain how this can be related to pedagogy:

> 'Learning strategy' can also be used as a tool to construct appropriate teaching methodologies, by permitting a consideration of specific cognitive techniques and how these might be best catered for. . . . 'Learning strategy' is a means for being specific about what is intended to be happening, cognitively, for the learner, that is, how the experience provided is expected to result in actual learning.

In a different article, Willing (1988b) emphasizes the *active* role of learners in the use of learning strategies. He goes on to state that "the term 'strategy' also contains the idea of a struggle or difficulty . . . the difficulty can only be coped with if an appropriate mode of attack is used" (p. 142).

2.1.1. Learning Strategies as Distinguished from Communication Strategies and Study Skills

Communication strategies are less directly related to learning and more related to the "process of participation in a conversation" (Rubin 1987:25). Oxford (1987), in her definition of communication strategies, focuses on the *compensatory* aspect of communication strategies—a feature which is very important in distinguishing these from learning strategies. Willing (1988b) talks of learning strategies as being "the comprehension, internalization, storing, and setting up of data accessible to the learner. On the other hand, the focus of communication strategies is the successful transmission and receiving of messages" (p. 147). However, he goes on to say that although traditionally in ESL these terms have been seen as belonging to different domains of discussion, in reality the terms most often overlap. For example, when a non-native speaker asks to have a word explained, this may be seen as a learning strategy or as a communication strategy. "Since communication strategies are, in part, techniques to enable communication, they necessarily function simultaneously as strategies of learning." Two pages later (p. 149), Willing makes his point even more explicitly: "For practical purposes in the language teaching context, a sharp distinction between these two notions would not in fact be useful."

A distinction is also made in the literature between learning strategies and *study skills*. Chamot and O'Malley (1987:242) relate the traditional and well-known teaching term of *study skills* to the notion of learning strategies: "Study skills describe overt behaviour such as taking notes. . . . Learning strategies . . . generally refer to mental processes which are not observable. Although this distinction . . . is important theoretically, we do not believe that it is always necessary to differentiate them in practice."

Drawing on the above, I have chosen to use the term *strategy* or *listening strategy* in this book, acknowledging the overlap between these terms.

2.1.2. Metacognitive and Cognitive Learning Strategies

The literature on learning strategies recurrently, and very consistently, distinguishes between two main types of learning strategies: "metacognitive" and "cognitive." In this section I will show how these different categories of strategies fit with my strategy-based approach.

Metacognitive strategies are defined as strategies "that can be used to regulate learning, i.e., plan, monitor and evaluate the range of cognitive strategies used to learn" (Wenden 1987:160). In my approach to teaching listening comprehension, I will be proposing that "reflection" (consciousness-raising, and developing metalinguistic and metastrategic awareness) and "regulation" (managing and monitoring) are essential if learners are to become good listeners.

An example of a metacognitive strategy particularly valuable for listening is developing a conscious awareness of the strategies listeners are using. Cognitive strategies, on the other hand, are techniques for managing particular materials being learned. They are much more closely tied to a specific situation or learning task and may not be applicable in others.

Examples of cognitive strategies in second-language listening would be note-taking, and listening for particular appelatives or honorific titles as clues to meaning.

As will be evident in the latter part of this book, there are strategies of both kinds being recommended. And, as Brown and Palincsar (1982) point out, the "ideal training package" requires a combination of metacognitive and cognitive strategies, as I have done.

2.1.3. The Growth of Interest in Learning Strategies and the "Good Language Learner" Literature

The literature on learning strategies has increased dramatically over the past ten to twenty years, and key books and articles are cited throughout this book. Notable examples related directly to ESL are Rubin, 1981; Stewner-Manzanares, Chamot, O'Malley, Kupper, and Russo, 1983; Wenden and Rubin, eds., 1987; Willing, 1989; O'Malley and Chamot, 1990; Oxford, 1990; Cohen, 1991; and Rost and Ross, 1991. In addition, books are beginning to appear on the market for "lay consumers"—language learners—advising them what strategies they can use to improve their language learning, and providing tips for language learning that they should try during their language course; for example, see H. D. Brown, 1989 and 1991; Willing, 1989.

This learning strategy literature, in turn, draws on research on "the good language learner" (notably Rubin 1975; Stern 1975; Naiman, Frohlich, Stern, and Todesco 1978; Stevick 1989). In this research, the intent is to identify and isolate what "the good language learner" does, and then devise ways to get poor language learners to do the same.

Some words of caution should be sounded when talking about strategy training and attempting to apply this principle. Everyone has strategies that they use, and some are more successful than others. Therefore, our basic premise should not be that students do not know how to do something and we will show them, but rather, as Porte (1988) puts it, we hope to show them ways to do it even better—after all, even a maestro can learn to play his or her instrument just a little better.

An additional caveat is that empirical studies have shown that good language learners often do quite different things. Stevick (1989:xi) states the following in the preface to his insightful book which analyzes the success of seven exceptional language learners:

> When I began the interviews, I was hoping to find out what the successful learners did alike. If we could teach their secrets to our students, I thought, then everyone else could become as successful as the people I had talked with. It soon became apparent, however, that learners are even more different from one another than I had expected.

Stevick's comments are an important warning that we not demand of this kind of inquiry answers that it cannot yield, and that we are cautious in our interpretation of findings. That notwithstanding, some recurrent patterns do emerge from the "good language learner" research, and this, plus the learning strategy literature, certainly provide some important insights. When examined judiciously, these insights can help us plan our teaching, and hence enhance our students' learning. The following are drawn, to a large extent from Rubin, 1975; Omaggio, 1978; and Stevick, 1989.

Good language learners possess the following characteristics:

i. Insight into their own learning style.

ii. Willing and accurate guessing.

iii. Lack of inhibition and a willingness to take risks and make mistakes in order to learn and communicate.

iv. Tolerance of the new language and the new systems in it and a willingness to live with a certain amount of vagueness.

v. Attendance to form—constantly looking for patterns in the language, and the way pieces of language are put together.

vi. Active approach to learning.

vii. Willingness to practice, taking a lot of trouble to spend time with speakers of the language being learned, and steer the interaction in directions that will enable them to practice.

viii. Attendance to the relationship of the participants and to the mood of the speech act.

ix. A view of language as serving many functions and knowledge that in any social interaction, there is room for interpretation of the speaker's intention. They know that many cues to the message are to be found in observing the nature of the interaction.

x. A willingness to try to isolate those features which give maximum intelligibility.

2.2. Learning Styles

Carver (1984:124) defines learning style as follows: "This category [learning style] is concerned with the learner's preferences for ways of organizing his learning, and with the interaction between his personality and his situation as a learner."

Keefe (1979:4) defines learning styles as "cognitive, affective, and physiological traits that are relatively stable indicators of how learners perceive, interact with, and respond to the learning environment."

It is important to note that these are relatively stable indicators, and not something totally permanent. As Reid (1987) points out, the important implication of this feature of learning styles is that they *can* be modified. In fact, as Schmeck (1981, cited by Reid, 1987:100) shows, "many individuals can change their strategies in response to the unique contextual demands of the instruction, the context, and the task." This has very important implications in providing theoretical justification for the strategy-based approach to the teaching of listening comprehension that I am advocating: "Subconscious learning styles can become conscious learning strategies" (Reid 1987:101). This, then, provides the link between learning styles and learning strategies.

Students must be helped to identify their individual learning styles. Reid (pp. 110–111) provides a very interesting "Perceptual Learning Style Preference Questionnaire." Using this questionnaire in her study, she finds that the nonnative speakers' preferred learning styles differ significantly from the native speakers.' However, it is important to heed Reid's warning not to make far-reaching assumptions and plans based on an analysis of the learners' learning styles, because there is a large number of intervening/confounding variables that have to be borne in mind such as motivation and the relationship between teacher and student. "In short, learning style preferences of students cannot be the sole basis for designing instruction" (p. 102).

2.3. Learning Strategies and Listening Strategies

Learning strategy research should be applied to virtually all aspects of ESL education in all the skill areas. This is certainly true for listening comprehension. See Oxford (1990:317–320) for an excellent list of strategies that are useful for listening. In Chapter 3, the principles underlying this approach, including such issues as whether or not to teach strategies explicitly, are developed, but it is helpful to point out some of the basic principles here.

2.3.1. Good ESL Learners Use a Lot of Strategies

Chamot (1987) examines the learning strategies of good ESL students, and finds two very important facts that support the argument for applying strategy training principles to listening: First, "the fact that students identified as good language learners . . . do use conscious learning strategies not only in ESL classrooms but also in nonclassroom acquisition environments is an indication that teachers could profitably direct students to utilize learning strategies for a variety of language learning activities" (p. 81). This does not necessarily imply that poor language learners are inactive, but rather that they might not utilize their strategies effectively or appropriately.[5] Second, Chamot (1987) finds that students reported far more strategy use in such areas as pronunciation and vocabulary than in listening and speaking. This would suggest that there is need for a lot of help in strategy training in listening.

---

[5] See also Murphy 1987; Chamot and Kupper 1989; Vann and Abraham 1990; Rost and Ross 1991.

2.3.2. A Strategy-Based Approach Makes Learning How to Listen More Effective

Spearrit (1962:5), discussing training native speakers in how to listen, states, "There is considerable evidence to indicate that instructional courses in listening lead to improvement in listening comprehension."

Learners need to be actively, consciously, and deliberately involved in their learning. They should be made aware of how the learning takes place, and what strategies will facilitate this. The application of research on learning strategies has an obvious and essential place in the classroom: I believe that *consideration of the strategies for listening comprehension should provide the backbone of any good listening comprehension course for second-language learners*. It provides the answer to the "how to" that I have been calling for. Wenden (1983:117) makes this point very forcefully:

> There is a need for curricular strategies, techniques, and materials to provide training that would not only expand learners' repertoires of efficient strategies but also make them aware of various aspects of their language learning and critically reflective of what they are aware—in effect, to refine the reflective phases of their language learning.

2.4. Classifications of Second-Language Learners' Listening Strategies

In this section I will attempt to present some of the most important listening strategies identified by different researchers in the recent literature.

As will become evident, although the classifications and terminology vary, there is a great deal of similarity between them.

2.4.1. Murphy (1987)

Murphy analyzed the listening strategies of ESL college students. His analysis is based on "think-aloud" protocols. He had students interact with the listening texts and talk about what they were doing and thinking, and how they were going about their listening. He came up with twelve strategies in four broad strategy groupings. His four strategy groupings, in order of their frequency of occurrence are Recalling, Speculating, Probing, and Introspecting.

Recalling involves paraphrasing textual information by the learners, putting what they have heard into their own words. This indicates that learners are attempting to recall what they heard as exactly as they can. Murphy identifies three recalling strategies:

i. *Paraphrasing*—rephrasing the information.

ii. *Revising*—learners are changing their minds and correcting themselves concerning some information they may have misunderstood the first time they heard it.

iii. *Checking*—checking when recalling information in order to support or verify something they had already introduced in their own comments.

Speculating involves introducing "listener-based information"—it goes well beyond "recalling." Listeners are using their imagination to help them in their listening. Murphy identifies four speculating strategies:

i. *Inferring*—listening between the lines, pulling separate pieces of textual information together or synthesizing.

ii. *Connecting*—drawing associations between what they hear and what they already know (note the importance of prior knowledge). Murphy cites the example of an informant who hears a textual reference to the Egyptian pyramids as being one of the seven wonders of the world, and who proceeds to speak about the other wonders of the world that she knows of, and that are part of her prior knowledge.

iii. *Personalizing*—listeners personalize their responses—they make a connection with what they already know as with connecting, but here they draw connections from their private lives or personal world view, whereas with connecting, the information would be commonly available as general knowledge. For example, the text is about nervous personality types, and one of the informants connects what he hears to his mother's boss and the man's behavior.

iv. *Anticipating*—listeners attempt to predict information that might be introduced at some future point in time. For example, an informant hears a text about packing up the treasures from King Tut's tomb, and says, "I think they are probably going to put those things they discovered into a museum. They're British so maybe the things they discover will go into a museum in England. . . ."

Probing involves going beneath the surface of the information presented. Murphy identifies three probing strategies:

i. *Analyzing the topics*—trying to find out more information than has been presented to them by such means as asking questions. Murphy cites examples of questions that go well beyond the material in the text and that indicate that listeners will focus their interpretation of the listening text on those issues for which they were asking questions. For example, when listening to a text on heart disease, one informant said, "I'm interested in something else. I want to know what are some of the symptoms . . ."

ii. *Analyzing the conventions of language*—focusing on specific features of the linguistic system such as definitions of words, pronunciation, and cohesive ties. It is important to note that Murphy identifies a significant difference between the linguistic focus of the more proficient and the less proficient listeners. The more proficient listeners focused on signals of rhetorical organization and structure of the text, while the less proficient group focused on meaning and pronunciation of unfamiliar words.

iii. *Evaluating the topics*—listeners make comments which are judgments or critical assessments concerning the information they have heard, for example contesting what they heard, based on what they knew to be the case. One informant challenged what was said in the text about the epidemic proportions of heart disease, by relating it to a different reality in her home country: "I know that not many people get heart disease because in my home country . . ."

Introspecting involves listeners focusing their attention inward and reflecting on their own experiences as listeners to the selections. Murphy identifies two introspecting strategies:

i. *Self-evaluating*—comments that show that learners are trying to keep track of how well they are doing while engaged in listening, e.g., "This is really too hard for me . . ." or "I understand that completely, but I think I already knew most of it before she explained it."

ii. *Self-describing*—students explain something about how they listen or what they are trying to do as they listen, e.g., "I said to myself, 'Well I missed this the first time' but now I remember . . ." or "It all came back to me on the way home . . ."

Murphy found that those students identified by an external criterion as more proficient listeners used more of the above strategies, and more frequently.

2.4.2. Willing (1987)

Willing is not writing specifically on listening comprehension, but several of the "information management strategies" described are valid and important for listening. He sees learning strategies as a means of information control—a means of learners avoiding becoming overloaded and overwhelmed. The strategies of this type that Willing identifies that specifically relate to listening are as follows:

Selectively attending involves focusing on the main points according to different criteria, which results in a reduction of the information load. As I have already said, this is an essential strategy if listeners are to avoid becoming overwhelmed. However, there is much more to be gained from selective attending: If students learn to listen selectively for the stressed words, this will lead them to a telegraphic version of the message. This will be addressed in more detail in several of the later chapters.

Associating, and thereafter keeping things which share some features together, is a very important cognitive process: keeping together items sharing a semantic field such as words all related to marriage; or features that share an affective tone such as anger tones. As Willing states, "This strategy takes information in and merges it with what has already been internalized . . . in this way the person places the information under his control" (p. 281). This process of associating relates directly to the notion of activating prior knowledge when listening.

Recognizing patterns involves recognizing, matching and reproducing patterns. Willing argues that this recognition of patterns is basic to learners maintaining control of the input. Although Willing is referring mainly to syntactic patterns, I would broaden this notion to the recognition of patterns of discourse (genres), and knowing how something being listened to is organized rhetorically. By recognizing patterns when listening, learners are able to make analogies which will assist in the guessing of meaning.

Analyzing involves the extraction of particular features from a given context. Here learners are perceiving a particular part of the pattern which can then be moved or manipulated through categorizing or inferencing.

Categorizing is based on analyzing—the extracted features are used to form concepts and groups.

Inferencing consists of discovering a solution by deriving it from what is already known. It involves comprehension of the meaning of the discourse beyond that which is explicitly stated. This involves bringing together different parts of the known plus prior knowledge, enabling learners to understand that which is inferred. In order to be a competent listener, it is essential to be able to make inferences. Take, for example, the following dialogue between a parent and a child:

> Parent: How did you do in the History test?
> Child: Ms. Panzerotti's tests are always unfair.

Competent listeners know that the inference is that the child did poorly.

2.4.3. O'Malley, Chamot, Stewner-Manzanares, Kupper, and Russo (1985)

In their 1985 study, O'Malley et al. were examining the learning strategies used by beginning and intermediate ESL students, not specifically for listening.

In this study, they came up with twenty-six strategies, nine metacognitive, sixteen cognitive, and one social mediation. Many of these are covered in the taxonomies of Murphy and Willing above. The comments that follow will relate specifically to aspects of the taxonomy that add to those given above and are germane to listening comprehension.

In the metacognitive category, an interesting addition to Willing's *selectively attending*, (which O'Malley et al. have a parallel for), is *directed attention*: "deciding in advance to attend in general to a learning task and to ignore irrelevant distractors." This is very important in listening comprehension, but it can only be utilized in ESL listening classes if learners know in advance of hearing the text what they should be directing their attention to. The inclusion of this strategy as separate from *selective attention* provides support for my claim that in teaching listening comprehension, we should make students aware of what it is they are going to be asked, and what they should specifically be listening for in the text. If what we are listening to is at all important, we usually know what we are listening for.

O'Malley et al. create the *cognitive* category of *note-taking*, which has obvious implications for listening in an academic and even in a nonacademic setting. An additional cognitive strategy that is particularly important to listening and not spelled out in the same detail in the previous taxonomies is *imagery*: "relating new information to visual concepts in memory via familiar, easily retrievable visualizations, phrases, or locations."

2.4.4. O'Malley, Chamot, and Kupper (1989)

This study, titled "Listening Comprehension Strategies in Second Language Acquisition" is *extremely* useful when advocating a strategy-based approach. My approach builds on precisely the kinds of insights that this study provides as to what effective and ineffective learners do when they listen. The findings are based on "think-aloud" protocols.

Three of the strategies which were found to be important in listening comprehension also yielded significant differences between the effective and ineffective listeners: *self-monitoring*, *elaboration* (relating new information to prior knowledge or to other ideas in the new information), and *inferencing*.

Effective listeners *listened for larger chunks* rather than on a word-by-word basis. As O'Malley, Chamot, and Kupper point out, this is "top-down" processing, and effective listeners used both top-down and bottom-up strategies, while ineffective listeners "became embedded in determining the meanings of individual words" (bottom-up).

An important observation made in this study which links directly with notions of "correctness" for comprehension, is that the effective listener is "adept at constructing meaningful sentences from the input he receives, even though the meaning *may be slightly different from the actual text*" [my emphasis].

Effective listeners made use of *prior knowledge* in three ways: they used their *world knowledge*, their *personal knowledge*—which created something meaningful for them—, and carried out *self-questioning*: "asking oneself questions about the material . . . or anticipating possible extensions of the information" (cf. Murphy, above).

2.4.5. Rubin (1988)

This study is much more classroom-oriented than the others cited in this section. However, it is valuable to note two strategies not captured by the other studies cited, which were found to be valuable for listening comprehension.

Rubin's *storyline strategy* is used while watching a video. Users try to determine the main plot or storyline. Clearly this is an extension of predicting, but the important addition for our purposes is that learners are trained not only to try to use the spoken language, but *also to concentrate on the visual material*, i.e., a nonlinguistic feature. Strategies of this type will be described in Chapter 6.

Rubin also trains her learners to use what she calls the *cognate strategy*. Listeners are encouraged to notice that an individual word or phrase sounds like one or more words in their own language. For example, they might hear the word "television" or "supermarket" and recognize that this word has been loaned into their language from English. This results in the formation of a hypothesis which is either validated or negated, usually through the visuals.

The latter chapters of this book describe classroom applications of what has been discussed in the abstract so far, and will reflect these ideas and incorporate the types of strategies identified and listed above.

2.5. Toward Learner Autonomy

It would be wise to begin by defining the term "autonomy" and "being autonomous" as it applies to learning. Holec (1985:88), a researcher who has written extensively on autonomy in second-language learning and self-directed learning, offers the following definition: "Being autonomous . . . is the capacity to run one's own learning affairs: it is a capability, a potential." As has already been stated, I see this as one of the major goals of any teaching: contributing toward the learner achieving autonomy. This is not an easy goal to achieve, nor is it an easy ideal for the teacher to live by. The reason for this is that we teachers are more accustomed to being cast in the role of being "all-knowing"—kind of living, walking, "reference tool." But, our aim is not self-gratification, and, therefore, we must devote our teaching to training students in the use of strategies that they can apply when on their own, and thereby learn on their own. This, in turn, will provide students with the tools to learn on their own. What is more, we must work toward a goal of *withdrawing our support*, however hard it might be to let go. We must help students to let go, and not encourage them to lean on us.

Another dimension of this notion of "autonomy" is that students should not get a sense that they are being "dictated to" as to what strategy to use and when. They should be made aware of what strategies they are and are not using, and what other strategies, found useful by others, are available to them.

Oxford, Lavine, and Crookall (1989:36) capture this idea very well:

> It is accurate to state that as a strategy trainer, the teacher becomes instrumental in helping each student to develop the self-awareness of how he or she learns, as well as the knowledge and means to maximize all learning experiences, even outside of the language learning area. Perhaps the greatest benefit derived from training in language learning strategies is that such training helps to provide a framework which can successfully be utilized in any learning situation.

The goal in our teaching is to effect a modification in the behavior of our students. If our input in the listening classes does not result in such a modification of the behavior of our students—in their ability to tackle listening tasks in the future—then I believe that we have failed. In the traditional approach to listening (characterized below as "testing" and not "teaching"), there certainly was *no* attempt to modify behavior!

2.6. The Impact of Strategy Training on Teaching

There is an added bonus to teaching learning strategies: it causes teachers to examine their *teaching* strategies (Cohen 1992). And what is more, such an approach causes teachers to give thought to their teaching style and approach and the learning styles of their students. This has been found to be very significant in successful classroom learning.

How, then, can we best describe the role of the teacher, given the above? Griffin (1981:38) offers a succinct and poignant answer to this question. She states that our starting point should be to ask, "What is happening in the learner right now, and how can I help best?" This is a far cry from the traditional role of the teacher. Hosenfeld (1979:52) captures the same concept by talking of a shift in focus from, "What must the teacher do to produce a given level of proficiency?" to "What must the student do to attain a given level of proficiency?" The focus has shifted from teacher to learner. And this is precisely the shift that is necessary if teachers are to use a strategy-based approach for the teaching of listening comprehension.

Perhaps the clearest statement of the role of the teacher that I have found is this: "Part of the mission of the adult educator is to train self-directed learners" (Wenden 1983:108, citing Knowles 1970 and Kidd 1973).

This shift in focus fits in very well with the role of the teacher in the Communicative model of second-language teaching: "The expert instructor becomes more of an advisor, manager, resource person, facilitator, and communicator" (Oxford, Lavine, and Crookall 1989:35). In fact, what becomes very clear is that a strategy-based approach not only "works" in a Communicative model, but it complements whatever else the teacher does, and contributes greatly to communicative competence.

2.7. The Main Goals of Teaching Listening Comprehension

As has already been stated, the past few years have seen a large increase in the recognition of the importance of explicitly teaching listening comprehension to ESL students. With improvement in international communications, and ever-increasing international trade, travel, and student exchange, students have become acutely aware of the vital importance of listening comprehension.

Teachers recognized this need, and have, to a large extent, abandoned the "osmosis" theory of listening comprehension (students picking up how to become competent listeners without any training).

33

Much of what we need to train our students to do when listening in a second language can be summed up by saying that students should be doing what they do when listening in their *first* language. This would include guessing anything that is not comprehended/heard, predicting what is to come, working out the meaning of unfamiliar/unheard terms from the context, and making inferences as to what is meant but left unsaid. It must, however, be borne in mind that much of what we do in our first language is not conscious, and consequently, one of our tasks is to bring to a conscious level what we do, and then try to get the students to apply the same strategies in the second language.

As mentioned above, a very important strategy we use when we listen in our first language is not listening to every word. We know the signals that point to what is of crucial importance (e.g., stress and slower speech) and what we can safely pay little attention to, and therefore deliberately listen to certain parts of an utterance more carefully than others. Gillian Brown (1987:280) calls this "prediction and sampling." She goes on to concede that such an approach might sometimes lead students to misinterpret, but she adds this: "So, after all, do native speakers [misinterpret]—I suspect far more than we ever imagine or need to check up on. We all get by with a rough fit with reality."

Gillian Brown (1977:168), as the conclusion to her book, provides what I consider to be the best statement of the goal of teaching listening comprehension:

> The main aim in teaching students how to understand English as it is normally spoken by native English speakers must be to make the students aware of what signals they can depend on hearing in the stream of speech and to make them use these signals . . . and help him to predict when only the tip of the iceberg is apparent what the shape of the rest of the iceberg must be.

This statement contains within it two of the major components of a good listening course. The first is developing strategies to recognize the different signals provided in spoken English—for example, paralinguistic signals such as gesture and variation in speed of speech; extralinguistic signals such as background noise and visual clues; and linguistic signals such as recognizable lexical items or syntactic patterns. The second component is training students to apply all this for use in hypothesis-formation, prediction, and inferencing. For example, students need to be trained to link what they have understood to their world knowledge, to assist them in arriving at the meaning. These points are of major importance, and are developed at length in the latter part of this book.

In effect, Gillian Brown's statement brings us back to the notion that a listening course must teach students *"how to "*—students must not be required just to listen to a passage and answer questions on it (this would be testing not teaching). They need to understand the *process* of listening, and to be shown how to tackle this daunting task. It is teaching students "how to" that leads to greater student autonomy, which is clearly a major objective of any second-language course.

In summary, much of what I believe should compose a listening comprehension course involves training in using strategies— hence my term a "strategy-based approach," spelled out in the following chapter, and then exemplified in detail in the rest of this book.

The Case for a Strategy-Based Methodology: Applying the Theoretical Principles

3.1. Introductory Comments

In the previous two chapters, I spelled out some of the theoretical assumptions about learning, listening comprehension, and learning strategies. In this chapter, I will define and discuss what I have called a "strategy-based" approach to the teaching of listening comprehension, and this will be built on the assumptions that have already been stated.

3.2. The Overall Argument in Summary

A strategy-based approach to listening is designed on principles of top-down processing. This makes possible the conscious use of strategies. These strategies can be monitored by both students and the teacher, and are amenable to training by the teacher. This approach will result in learners becoming more confident in, and adept at tackling listening passages that at first might seem beyond their ability. Moreover, recognizing the value of using more strategies, and learning about additional strategies, will lead to greater learner autonomy.

3.3. Definition of a Strategy-Based Approach

As I argue repeatedly throughout this book, my basic belief regarding second-language pedagogy is that our role as teachers is to train our students *how to do something*. I believe that this is the foundation of *all* second-language pedagogy, regardless of the specific skill or skills, or whether the skills are being taught in an integrated manner or discretely. Exposure to spoken English is necessary, but not sufficient, if we are to help our students to become competent listeners. Faerch and Kasper (1986:264) argue that "comprehension takes place when input and knowledge are matched against each other." However, as O'Malley, Chamot, and Kupper (1989:422) point out, this match is seldom perfect, and special "mental processes are activated in order to understand." These mental processes are *learning strategies*.

It is my contention that when we design an ESL course, we are, in effect, attempting to address two questions. The first is, *What do we want our students to be able to do by the end of the course that they were unable to do at the beginning of the course?* The answer to this question defines for us the goal of the course. Having answered that, the second question is, *How, through our course, do we achieve that goal?* When this question is asked for listening comprehension, the answer is the following: *We achieve that goal by training our students to use all available strategies to assist them in getting at the meaning of what they are listening to, i.e., by using a "strategy-based" approach.*

A strategy-based approach, then, is a methodology that is rooted in strategy training (discussed in detail below). It is an approach that sees the objective of the ESL course as being to train students how to listen, by making learners aware of the strategies that they use, and training them in the use of additional strategies that will assist them in tackling the listening task. Chamot and O'Malley (1987:244) capture very clearly the relationship between learning strategies and my strategy-based approach:

> Suggestions for learning strategy instruction include showing students how to apply the strategies, suggesting a variety of different strategies for the language and content tasks of the curriculum, and providing many examples of learning strategies throughout the curriculum so that students will be able to generalize them to new learning activities in other classes and even outside the classroom.

Learners have to be weaned away from strategies that are unhelpful or even destructive, like grabbing for a dictionary or panicking when an incomprehensible word is heard, and these have to be replaced by such helpful strategies as guessing the meaning of a word from the context. Of course, arguing for a strategy-based methodology does not negate the necessity for extensive exposure to, and practice in listening, but it defines what shape the listening comprehension course will take. Everything that I argue for when discussing the classroom applications and implementation of the strategy-based approach, is predicated on the assumption that listening, and, indeed any language learning, requires a great deal of practice.

Unfortunately, learner training and strategy-training are not yet seen as central to second-language teaching. As Wenden (1987) suggests, this is probably due to the as yet limited empirical proof of its effectiveness, and, I would argue, in larger measure due to the fact that most teachers are not clear as to how to apply such an approach, or precisely what a course following these principles would look like.

One very valuable study providing empirical support for the value of strategy training in listening is Rubin (1988). However, a word of caution based on O'Malley's (1987) findings on strategy training for listening is in order: For strategy training to be successful, it is essential that enough time be given for learners to become familiar with the strategies that they are being trained to use.

What I am proposing, then, is that a listening comprehension course for second-language learners should be virtually synonymous with the notion of *teach the learners strategies for listening*. As Willing (1988a:90) puts it, "If a strategy has been isolated and identified, it then becomes possible for teachers to teach that strategy as a skill." This approach, which I have been advocating for upward of a decade, ties in very well with the ever-growing body of research literature on learning strategies and the intriguing literature on the "good language learner." This literature provides a sound theoretical base for my strategy-based approach.

A strategy-based approach also links directly with the body of literature urging that second-language pedagogy strives toward the goal of learner autonomy. This, in turn, requires that learners learn how to learn, and that we, the teachers, assist them in achieving this. Learner autonomy is the larger goal of any ESL course, and a good strategy-based approach leads directly toward this goal.

3.4. Justification for the Teaching of Strategies

Strategy training can be justified, based on the following six propositions:

i.   *Strategies can be taught.* O'Malley (1987), alluding to the work of Krashen (1983), which argues that the major role of the second-language teacher is to provide "comprehensible input," suggests that the teacher can be of greater value than that, and should "embed" some strategies into the curriculum, which will increase the overall class performance (see also Cohen 1991).

ii. *Academic language learning is more effective with learning strategies.* Brown and Palincsar (1982:7) state that learner training should consist of "both practice in the use of task-appropriate strategies, instruction concerning the significance of those activities and instruction concerning the monitoring and control of strategy use." By learning to listen in a program using a strategy-based approach, not only do learners learn to apply the appropriate strategies, but their consciousness is raised, and they develop a metalinguistic awareness of how language functions and is learned.

iii. *Mentally active learners are better learners.* This notion was empirically tested by Chamot (1987). She found in her study that better students used more strategies inside and outside the formal language classroom. Drawing on this, she suggests that "intervention by the teacher could help less able students profit from the strategies used by more able students" (p. 81). This is evocative of the early literature on the "good language learner," which aimed at identifying the strategies of good learners so that they could be taught to poor learners.

iv. *Learning strategies transfer to new tasks.* This notion can even be taken beyond "new tasks," ultimately working toward learner autonomy. Learner autonomy has two aspects to it. First, it involves becoming an active learner in control of the learning, rather than a passive vessel into which information should be "poured" by the teacher. Second, such strategy training provides learners with the tools to continue to grapple with the language being learned long after their formal language classes are over.

v. *Strategies facilitate "information management."* Strategies are a way language learners handle the enormous quantity of information "coming at" them (Willing 1988b:146). Without applying effective strategies, learners would soon become overwhelmed, and probably "tune out." This, too, is a very powerful rationale for strategy training and a strategy-based approach to second-language learning.

vi. *Strategy training teaches learners how to learn.* As Cohen (1990:1) points out, this need to learn how to learn is far from obvious: "We would not think of undertaking many of our lifelong pursuits without coaching or formal training. . . . Yet when it comes to learning a target language, we usually do not have a coach to help us *learn* more effectively." Only recently has this issue really come to the fore in second-language pedagogy.[6]

Recently there have been some very interesting attempts to face this issue head-on. An interesting example is a student ESL text by Ellis and Sinclair (1989a) plus Teacher's Book (1989b), *Learning To Learn English: A Course In Learner Training.* They set up their book in two stages: Stage One—"Preparation for Language Learning," which develops metacognitive strategies; and Stage Two—"Skills Training," which includes a mix of metacognitive and cognitive strategies (for further example, see Willing 1989).

3.5. Metalinguistic Awareness

Many students learning second languages are unaware of how language functions—they lack metalinguistic awareness. Metalinguistic awareness is defined by Brown and Palincsar (1982:3) as "the ability to step back and consider one's own thought (or language) as itself an object of thought and to use the subsequent conceptualization to direct and redirect one's cognitive theories." Metalinguistic awareness is particularly important to second-language learners because it helps them to make meaningful and helpful comparisons between the situation in their first language and the situation in the language being learned (Sharwood-Smith 1981). In addition, this awareness encourages

---

[6] See also Holec (1981); Riley (1982); Crookall (1983); Prowse (1983); Oxford (1990)— particularly Oxford's eight-step strategy-training model.

students to self-correct, and may even be important for self-monitoring (Gass 1983).

It is interesting to note that Chamot (1987) found that her subjects, all of whom were designated by their teachers as "good" language learners, displayed a remarkably high degree of metalinguistic awareness. They also displayed a high degree of sophistication in their ability to describe their use of a wide range of learning strategies.

The development of "meta-awareness"—metalinguistic awareness, together with metastrategic awareness (discussed below), is essential in my strategy-based approach to the teaching of listening comprehension.

3.6. Metastrategic Awareness

As is the case with awareness about language, many students are unaware of the power of strategies for facilitating their learning and comprehension. They know very little about the *process* of language learning—they lack what I call "metastrategic awareness." The development of such an awareness assists learners to "focus their learning" (see Rubin 1987). I see one of the major responsibilities of the teacher as being to develop learners' awareness of the strategies they use, the strategies they could add, and the value of strategies. The teacher must develop in each learner an awareness of how he or she learns, and suggest additional and/or alternative strategies when those that the student is using do not appear to be working well. Learners will "buy into" this strategy training if they see the significance and effectiveness of these strategies.

The way in which I introduce and begin to develop this awareness is by playing a game with students. They listen to snippets of recordings in a language that they do not know at all. I tell them that this is a game, and that they should not expect to understand everything. What they are asked to do is to listen to each snippet, and to write down what they think they are listening to, and, more importantly, to write down *what they based their decision on*. After they have heard all the snippets, we hold a discussion, and very quickly the students realize that with some of the snippets they managed quite well, and then we discuss how this was possible, and they come to realize that tone of voice, background noise, speed of speech, etc., provide the basis for an educated guess which is often fairly accurate. Having convinced them that they were even able to "understand" something in a language they did not know at all, I then repeat the exercise, this time using a very difficult English passage (Mendelsohn 1992). This kind of activity is very convincing, and paves the way for subsequent strategy training.[7]

The development of this metastrategic awareness is the first step in training students as to what other strategies they might apply. As Carver (1984) points out, this requires that learners be guided to describe the strategies that they use. Drawing on Allwright (1980), he advocates that this description should include the parameters of frequency of use, enjoyment, usefulness, and efficiency. Carver correctly emphasizes that this should not simply constitute a historical record, but should "serve as a way of recording possibilities of what a learner might do in the future" (p. 129).

3.7. Strategy Training

Training learners to use a larger number of more effective strategies will make them better learners—effective strategy use is an essential component of good learning. The idea is, then, that strategy training will lead to their more *active involvement* in the learning, itself leading to more efficient learning. What is more, this strategy training will increase learner autonomy. To achieve this goal, it is imperative that the teacher not merely be a provider of comprehensible input (Krashen 1983), but be a *strategy trainer* and train students to use different strategies. Such strategy training requires that the teacher, and more importantly, the learners themselves, become aware of the strategies that are being used and where the weaknesses lie, and then, on the basis of this, decide what can be done to improve the situation. Or, in other words, for strategy training to be really successful, students "need to know what the strategy is,... how to apply it . . . and when and where to use the strategy" (Jones et al. 1987:41). The teacher also has to determine which strategies would be most useful for any particular learning tasks and settings. Furthermore, decisions have to be made as to which strategies would be best suited to which students. Students, for their part, should be developing a flexibility in applying or choosing certain strategies. Moreover, the teacher should be encouraging students to try out new strategies—some students will like one particular strategy, others will like another. Strategies will not all "work" for everybody. Cohen (1990:190), addressing learners directly on this point says, "Experimenting to find out what works best can be a 'liberating' experience for you."

Having stated the value of strategy training (also known as "learner training"), I feel that it is important that we not go overboard in our claims for its importance. *Strategy training is not everything.* Naiman et al. (1978:99) also make this point in their "Good Language Learner" study: "It would be unwise to focus exclusively on learning strategies and techniques. This study . . . has confirmed the conviction that strategies and techniques form only a part of language learning. It is therefore important to relate them to personality and motivational factors in the learner, and to other less obvious aspects of the learning process."

The implementation of strategy training has to be carefully handled because, as Naiman et al. and Stevick have shown, "the successful or good language learner, with predetermined overall characteristics, does not exist. There are many individual ways of learning a language successfully" (Naiman et al. 1978:103).

---

[7] See Brown and Palincsar (1982:4-7) for additional discussion on making students aware in a strategy-training program.

A further caution about strategy training is that it is a powerful tool and, like all powerful tools, it is dangerous when handled carelessly. Strategy training handled too heavy-handedly, or imposed on learners who are doing well without these interventions, can have a negative effect. Care must therefore be taken as to how, when, how much, and with whom strategy training should take place. Teachers must find out what strategies their students are already using and build on them.

3.7.1. Planning the Strategy Training

Strategy training needs to be carefully planned. The following draws on Jones, Palincsar, Ogle, and Carr's (1987:64–70) extended example, and on Rubin (1988) for number (ii). While Jones et al.'s example is not from the domain of second-language teaching, the principles still hold:

i.   The teacher must analyze what strategies students already have available to them, and decide what other strategies would be helpful.

ii. The teacher must work out ways that these strategies can be taught.

iii. The teacher must devise ways to help students to identify the problems that they are having.

iv. The teacher must plan ways to link the new information to prior knowledge—usually through prelistening activities.

v.   The teacher must develop training activities in the use of the new strategies. This will involve training in the use of different strategies for different purposes when listening.

vi. The teacher must provide real listening activities with all supports and "crutches" removed. These will take the form of uncontrolled, real listening tasks.

Chamot and O'Malley's (1987) C.A.L.L.A. (Cognitive Academic Language Learning Approach) lesson plan is a good example of how strategy training can be incorporated into the teaching. Like Jones et al. above, they move from a stage in which the teacher is much more overtly and directly involved ("with scaffolding"), to a stage in which the teacher's role is diminished and, we hope, the students use the strategies independently.

There are a number of models for strategy training in the learning strategy literature, some for learning and strategy training in general, some specifically for second-language learning. Brown and Palincsar (1982:14) offer a brief and somewhat generalized model. An extremely valuable and detailed model for strategy training may be found in Jones et al. (1987:53–56). Oxford (in Wenden et al. 1989) also offers a very clear and detailed model for strategy training. It comprises the following steps: identifying the needs of learners, for example, time available; choosing the strategies for training; considering ways to integrate the training; considering affective issues like motivation; preparing materials and activities; conducting completely informed training; evaluating the learner training; and revising the training based on the evaluation.[8]

3.7.2. Preparing Students for Strategy Training

ESL students bring to their language learning a disparate set of notions about what learning and teaching should be like and "look" like, and what the roles of teacher and learners are. Very often these are dramatically different from our own beliefs, and even, sometimes, diametrically opposed to them. For example, many learners are used to a classroom situation in which the teacher, always at front and center stage, is active while the students are passive. Or, an even more difficult situation to tackle is learners who have been made to believe that they cannot learn on their own. When planning strategy training, these facts have to be taken into account, and students have to be prepared for the active and interactive part that they are going to be expected to play in their learning. Without this, there will be very serious resistance to the tasks and to the approach.

Students have to be aware of what it is that the teacher is doing and having them do and why. If they are involved in this enterprise and made to see its value and applications, they will be open to it and cooperate. They will then develop an ownership of the strategies and, we hope, retain them and apply them in the future.

In Section 3.6 I described a "precourse" consciousness-raising/ awareness-raising game. This can, in fact, be taken even further as Cohen does, with ongoing discussions with learners as to how they are doing, how they are feeling, etc., throughout their language program. Cohen reports how he met weekly with adult immigrants learning Hebrew in Israel, and discussed their language learning with them. This included a discussion of the different strategies that the learners had been using and their effectiveness (in Wenden et al. 1989 and Cohen 1990).

3.7.3. Should Strategy Training Focus on Cognitive or Metacognitive Strategies?

A good strategy-training program should be addressing both. And, what is more, they are interdependent—cognitive strategy training without metacognitive strategy training is unlikely to have much transfer value, even if it helped learners with specific problems. On the other hand, metacognitive strategy training without cognitive strategy training will probably not be very

---

[8] An additional example of an explicit strategy training model for second-language learning may be found in Wenden (1987:159-162 and 166).

well received by learners—it will appear very abstract, and not necessarily relevant to their immediate needs, and motivation to do something with this would likely be low. Wenden (1987:161) cites an example from listening comprehension that makes this very point: "It is of limited use to train language learners to monitor their progress in listening [metacognitive] if they do not have a repertoire of cognitive strategies necessary to deal with the difficulties they may perceive themselves to have." It should also be borne in mind that if the approach being advocated entails involving students and making them aware of what is being done and why, then this, ipso facto, will constitute the metacognitive part explaining the value, place, transferability, etc., of the cognitive strategies.

3.7.4. Should Strategy Training Be Explicit or Implicit?

I believe that there is more value to making the strategy training explicit than in keeping it implicit, although, as Willing (1988a) points out, empirical proof of this is not yet available. It is my contention that virtually all good second-language pedagogy should be strategy-based and that the metacognitive component of making learners aware of what they are doing and how this will contribute to the learning process is a necessary component. As Willing (1988a:97) puts it, "Virtually any class activity may be used to encourage the development of learning strategies. All that is necessary is to focus attention upon the learning-process aspect of an experience, which always exists side by side with the content. The learner needs to be able to discover the strategies underlying particular classroom activities." I am also firmly convinced that learners like to know *what* they are doing and *why*, and that this increases their commitment to the learning and makes them more willing to try, even if the procedure or approach is foreign to them. Without this, some of the tasks may be judged irrelevant by learners.

3.7.5. Should Strategy Training Be Separate From, or Integrated into the Regular Course?

A case can be made for both approaches, although I am advocating integrating the strategy training. Stated very simply, "the integrated training consists of teaching content teachers how to incorporate learning strategy instruction into their regular classrooms" (O'Malley and Chamot 1990:153). I have found that the transfer of strategies to new tasks is more likely when the strategy training is done in conjunction with the regular course.

Chamot and O'Malley (1987), in their C.A.L.L.A. Model described above, argue *for* embedding strategy training into the regular language work, making it an integral part of it and not an "appendage" of some sort, as Moulden's manual described below might have appeared.

Tyacke and Mendelsohn (1986) also advocate an "embedded" approach to strategy training in second-language teaching. What is more, this notion of embedding strategy training into the regular learning and making it an integral part of the regular learning is at the root of my strategy-based approach for learning to listen. I do not see strategy training as some sort of "add-on" or "trick" that can be used in emergencies, but rather as the essence of the teaching of listening comprehension in ESL. Embedding strategy training is completely compatible with making strategy training explicit, as discussed in Section 3.7.4 above. (For further discussion of this question, see Campione and Armbruster 1985; Wenden 1987.)

There are those who argue for keeping strategy training separate (Derry and Murphy 1986; Jones et al. 1987). However, in addition to my own classroom experience which argues to the contrary, Wenden's findings (1987) and Moulden's experience (1985) would argue against this.

Wenden's experiment in strategy training at Columbia University was rather unsuccessful. Clearly, part of the reason for this is because the materials used were not integrated. Discussing her experiment and the learners' negative attitude to it, she states, "These [negative] reactions suggested that the materials be more integrated in their approach. Therefore they were revised so that the concept and related set of skills highlighted by each module focus on a particular language learning task or objective, and continued use of the revised materials has proven to be more successful in involving the students."

Moulden (1985) carried out an experiment in self-directed learning with engineering students in Nancy, France, which was also enlightening on this point. The experiment included the preparation and use of a manual on how to learn (clearly not integrated with the language learning itself). Moulden's findings, like Wenden's, were disappointing, but mainly, I believe, for different reasons. However, from our point of view, what is interesting is to note the clear lack of enthusiasm of the students for the manual on how to learn. They reported that they did not gain much from it. This, then, would seem to be arguing against keeping that sort of training separate and unintegrated.

3.8. A Model Showing the Relationship Between Strategy Training and Mendelsohn's Strategy-Based Approach

Carver (1984) proposes a model for language learning which shows the place of learner strategies. His model is designed for the incorporation of learning strategies into a design for self-directed learning. However, this model fits extremely well with what I am proposing for listening comprehension, although mine is not a self-directed model.

Carver describes the learning of many learners as follows: a particular *learning style* produces certain kinds of *work habits*. He goes on to argue that what is very often missing is a reasoned *learning plan*. Learner strategies, according to Carver, "arise directly from learning styles and work habits, and so tend to be adventitious and unplanned" (p. 125). What is called for to improve this situation is *conscious plans*. "It is suggested that the outcome in the form of learner strategies may [as a result of the conscious plans] be more effective and more satisfying for the learner."

Carver's model for improved language learning may be shown as the following:

> learning styles—leading to—work habits—leading to—conscious plans

This model can be very easily applied to my strategy-based approach, and can be used to show what I am proposing.

As above, a particular *learning style* produces certain kinds of *work habits*. What I am proposing is also a *learning plan*, intended to make the experience more effective and satisfying for the learner. The learning plan in my model is the *strategy-based listening comprehension course*.

Mendelsohn's strategy-based model for learning to listen may be shown as the following:

> learning styles—leading to—work habits—leading to—a strategy-based listening course

3.9. Strategies in the Second-Language Listening Class

In this section I will relate the issue of strategies and strategy-training specifically to second-language listening comprehension.

In Mendelsohn (1984), I put forward the view that second-language learners often do not approach the listening task in the most efficient way despite what they may do in their first language. In fact, they often try to listen word-by-word and to understand everything—what Clarke (1980), writing about reading comprehension, calls "short circuiting" the good reader's system. Rubin (1975), endorsing the ideas of Twaddell (1973), says that learners must accept "temporary vagueness"—a situation that we are all very comfortable with in our first-language communication.

The fact that students do not approach their listening in the most efficient way is borne out by Chamot (1987), who found that students did not use a very large number of strategies when listening. There is a double irony to this reality. The first irony, of course, is that there are many strategies that second-language learners use, usually unconsciously, when listening in their *first* language, but do not transfer to the second-language listening. The second irony is that the unsuccessful way students go about second-language listening may be attributable in part to the kind of listening that they are traditionally required to do in ESL courses. In other words, this inefficient approach is partly teacher-induced. Students collect "phonological information in working memory, and then attempt an analysis" (Clark and Clark 1977, cited by Henner-Stanchina 1982) when what they should be doing is anticipating what is to come. This "limited system of comprehension" may be adequate for the artificial tasks [tests!] that follow the listening in traditional listening comprehension courses, but it is not adequate for real comprehension.[9]

In Section 1.6, I cited O'Malley, Chamot, and Kupper's excellent definition of listening comprehension (1989:434). The essential components of their definition are the following: listening is active and conscious; listeners use cues from the text together with their world knowledge; and the task of comprehending is achieved by using different strategies.

The detailed application of this comprehensive definition forms the substance of the remainder of this book. However, I would like to give a couple of examples, simply to illustrate these abstract ideas:

First, when second-language listeners are confronted with a word that they do not understand, they need to be encouraged to attempt to discern the meaning from the context. This has been conventional wisdom for a long time in the teaching of reading, but somehow has not been developed in the teaching of listening. Second, learners should be watching their interlocutor's face and body language, as these often provide clues to the meaning. As will be detailed later, these sorts of strategies need to be discussed with students, and activities need to be developed that will both train students and give them practice in using them.

---

[9] A notable exception to what has been done traditionally is Geddes (1988), whose course teaches students how to listen.

The Essential Features and Design of a Strategy-Based Listening Comprehension Course

4.1. Introductory Comments

This chapter attempts to cover the essential features, principles, and design of a strategy-based listening comprehension course. Much of what appears in this chapter should, I believe, guide the planning of *any* listening course. This chapter is particularly important, bearing in mind what is usually done in traditional ESL listening comprehension courses.

4.2. The Course Should Include a Large Amount of Listening

At first glance, this might seem too obvious a point to note. However, it is not. Often, in traditional listening comprehension courses, when listening was explicitly taught, an insufficient amount of listening took place to really be of benefit to learners. As the focus moves toward teaching students how to listen, care must be taken not to invest all the listening course time in talking *about* listening without allowing a large amount of time for actual listening.

4.3. The Material Should Be Spoken English

As was discussed above, there are significant differences between spoken and written English, which are overlooked in many traditional listening materials. There are many ways in which traditional listening materials lack naturalness (see Porter and Roberts 1981). One of the main problems is that the material is often a recording of a *reading* of *written* English. This puts a strain on second-language learners because of the greater density of content, the greater complexity of the syntax and the absence of the natural redundancy of the spoken language. In fact, second-language learners may be being asked to do something more difficult than the usual listening tasks of native speakers. What is more, such material fails to expose learners to real spoken English with its special features.

4.4. The Material Should Include Dialogue and Monologue

An examination of traditional listening comprehension materials for second-language learners reveals that a large proportion is *monologue*. This is ironic since most of what native listeners listen to in the real world is interactive *dialogue*. Therefore, care must be taken to assess the learners' listening needs, and to include both dialogue and monologue unless, for a special need, listening only to monologue needs to be practiced.

4.5. The Content Should Be Appropriate

The choice of what students will be expected to listen to is crucial. There are a number of factors to be taken into consideration in addition to those covered by, say, a needs analysis. For example, the age of the learners must be borne in mind, so that the material is neither too sophisticated nor too "young" for the students in question. If the material is perceived as being too young, this will have a negative effect and will appear patronizing however good the training and the activities are. For example, I have witnessed adult learners being expected to work on infantile stories—this resulted in much resentment.

Care must be taken that there is a "match" between the material being listened to and the task being given. Clearly, native speakers listen to different things in different ways (see Chapter 9), and teachers must be sure that the material they choose is appropriate for the types of questions and tasks that follow it. There are numerous examples in traditional listening comprehension courses in which there is a "mismatch." For example, students hear a fairly casual conversation between two friends but are then asked to answer questions on minute points of detail. Not only does this seldom occur in real life, but in most cases students do not know ahead of hearing the passage that they need to take note of such detail. Not only is this unrelated to reality, but it teaches students listening habits precisely of the type that we want to break—habits such as listening intently for every detail in all listening.

Care must always be taken, as has been stated, that most of the material be real, *spoken* English, with all that this implies, both in terms of the organization and content-density and in terms of the style and speed of delivery. This does not mean that *all* the material has to be "found" (existing, real) material. That would preclude some of the training activities that I will argue below are an essential part of a strategy-based approach—found material does not always lend itself to some of the focused training activities, and the quality of the recording might be problematic as well. What is more, particularly in the training stage, there may very well be situations in which it is desirable to control for a particular variable—for example, background noise—and this would not be possible working only with found materials. However, the listening course should always be working toward, and ultimately providing practice in listening to a lot of *real* language.

Finally, care must be taken to vary the content. However relevant the material, if it is too similar, it will lead to tedium, so a change from time to time is essential.

4.6. The Level of Difficulty Should Be Carefully Set

Determining the level at which to pitch a listening course, relative to the level of the students, is not a simple matter. In the audiolingual paradigm, listening was less for comprehension, and more to provide the basis for pattern practice. The level was to be low enough that students would be able to make the necessary responses correctly, virtually all of the time, as they were going through the process of habit formation, and one had to ensure that the habits being formed were correct! When the goal of a listening course is, as I have suggested, to help students *comprehend spoken English for real communication*, then a different approach to leveling has to be taken. I would propose following the principle advocated by Krashen (1983)—that the course be pitched at the level of "i + 1," where "i" is the level at which the students stand. In other words, the material should be one notch above the students' comfort level so that they are suitably challenged, and so that they can learn to comprehend at this level by means of the prudent use of strategies.

Having made such a determination in principle, we still need to grapple with an even more difficult issue: What determines the level of difficulty of an existing piece of listening? There are many variables to be taken into consideration:

i.   *The length of the listening passage.* The longer the passage, the more difficult it is for second-language learners to "hold it together." A longer passage is often overwhelming to them, largely because they are not using strategies that guide them as to what is of major and what is of minor importance—the "wood" is being lost for the "trees." What is more, in a longer passage, students may need to piece together information that is not all taken from the same section in the listening, or is only comprehensible by inference, and this makes for a much harder task.

ii. *How well or poorly the passage is organized.* Another major factor that affects the difficulty level of a listening text is its rhetorical organization. Anderson and Armbruster (1984) make the distinction between "considerate" text and "inconsiderate" text. Jones et al. (1987:12), using these terms, describe text as *considerate*, "when the text structure and the genre fit the writer's [in our case the speaker's] purpose, are well-signaled by cue words, have cohesion and unity of theme, and are audience appropriate in terms of content and vocabulary." *Inconsiderate* text is defined as "text that is difficult to understand because it is poorly organized and poorly written; it may be incoherent, lack signal words, have inappropriate text structures, or have vocabulary that is too dense and inappropriate for the age level."

iii. *How skilled the speakers are.* Some speakers are clearer and better organized, and make greater use of paralinguistic features to underscore or confirm their words. These speakers are much easier to comprehend, and this can make a significant difference to the second-language learner's comprehension.

iv. *Explicitness of information.* Anderson and Lynch (1988:50–54) point out that in listening, this is a significant variable. They divide this explicitness into the following: the amount of redundancy—whether the speaker provides all the necessary information but no more—and "whether the hearer is required to recognize alternative expressions referring to the same character." (See also Chiang and Dunkel 1992).

v. *Familiarity with the speakers' dialect.* Students have greater difficulty with dialects of English which they are unfamiliar with. It is true that native speakers find it more difficult, but they very quickly "tune in" to the unfamiliar dialect and make the necessary accommodations as they listen.

vi. *Speed of delivery.* In our first language, we are able to comprehend speech delivered at a far greater rate than average speech, but still the level of comprehension has been found to drop when the rate of delivery is above average (above 150 words per minute—Spearrit 1962). In a second language, this is an even more crucial factor, and overly rapid delivery can throw students off completely and cause them to give up. It should, however, be noted that this is *not* a call for overly or unnaturally slow speech, either (see below).

vii. *The amount of extralinguistic and paralinguistic signals.* These signals assist listeners with comprehending the words. Examples are background noise, markers of location, and gesture. Gillian Brown and George Yule (1983:86) discuss the importance of the presence or absence of the "visual environment," and how helpful it is to watch a speaker's face, body movement, etc.

viii. *Familiarity with the topic.* Clearly this is an important factor. As was described in Section 1.3 when discussing schema theory and prior knowledge, studies have shown that this will impact dramatically on how difficult or easy a listener finds a particular listening passage.

ix.   *The level of interest.* A final factor which is very important to second-language listeners is whether they have interest in the material. Students will do better if the material is interesting and relevant to them.

Spearrit (1962:9) claims that for native speakers, "the amount of material comprehended is also likely to be influenced by the perceived prestige of the speaker." While I have no empirical basis to argue against Spearrit's claim, my extensive classroom experience with second-language speakers has not borne this out.

Many of the factors listed above may be modified in order to make a listening *passage* easier or more difficult. In addition, when designing a listening comprehension course, it is important to bear in mind that the level of difficulty can also be varied by raising or lowering the level of the task assigned on the same piece of listening (Anderson and Lynch 1988).

4.7. The Delivery, i.e., the Recording, Should Be Natural

Traditionally in ESL listening courses, the pronunciation is deliberate and artificial—words are too clearly enunciated, and delivery is unnaturally slow when the speech should be natural. In such cases, features which characterize fast speech, such as assimilation of similar sounds and deletion of certain sound segments, are not present, and this can have the effect of leaving students with the false impression that this is how English is really spoken, and, what is more, that using the fast speech rules is a sign of slovenly and even substandard English. And, worst of all, this fails to prepare learners for real listening. As Dunkel (1986) points out, there is an abundant availability of authentic materials of all sorts, so there is no reason to disadvantage students in this way. It is encouraging to note that things are changing—Kellerman (1992a) identifies a major emphasis on authenticity of text in her survey of recent British listening materials.

The overall speed of delivery is often exaggeratedly slow—something that might in the short term be comforting to students, but will not help them in the long term. Blau (1990) found that if, for pedagogic reasons, it is desirable to modify the delivery of a passage in order to make it more comprehensible, then the effective way to do this is by inserting pauses at constituent boundaries, not to slow the speech down and eliminate the fast-speech features.

At the suprasegmental level, the problem is even more acute: If intonation is exaggerated, the material is usually chunked into units which are not as closely tied to the structure of the information being conveyed as they should be. Even more problematic is the fact that such abnormal delivery tends to obscure the distinction between that which should be stressed and that which should be unstressed, because so much overstressing occurs. Even words that would normally be unstressed acquire some stress. As will be discussed in Chapter 7, learning to identify stress/unstress is a very useful strategy when attempting to ascertain the main idea of what is being listened to, but this is only possible when the stress/unstress is "natural."

The syntax, too, is often pedantically correct and "complete." For example, traditional materials are noticeable for the absence of "short answers" like "Yes" or "Yes, he did." Instead, these materials abound in "ESL English" such as "Yes, he did know the answer," in answer to the question, "Did he know the answer?" Needless to say, a grunt of agreement, or merely a nod of the head (on video) are even more rare in such materials.

Also noticeably absent are hesitation phenomena, abandoned half-sentences, talk-over, etc. These are often carefully edited out, depriving ESL learners of exposure to language as it is normally spoken. Learners can usually identify the nonverbal sounds such as "mmm" or "um." However, when the speaker is using real English words as a means of playing for time, for example, by saying, "Well, in effect, to be perfectly honest . . ." or starts a sentence and abandons it half-way, this can really "throw" learners.

Another factor that needs to be considered when teaching listening comprehension, is differences in accents. While I believe that it is correct to pitch most of the material at a "middle-of-the-road" type accent, in a course for intermediate to advanced learners, it is valuable to provide exposure to a range of different accents.

All of the above mentioned points on naturalness suggest that we need to be very cautious about materials prepared specially for second-language learners. What is more, when possible, I would strongly recommend the use of video over audio recordings. When discussing strategies and strategy training, I will be advocating training students to watch for facial expressions, gesture, clothing, items in the background, etc., that will provide clues to meaning. Much of what can help them is visual and is lost in the more artificial medium of audio recording. This in turn makes the listening task much harder than real listening.

This leaves the question of live presentations. There is always something more artificial in a recording than if the presentation is live. Comprehension with live presentations was found to be easier in a study done with native speaking children by Caffrey (1955), who found that the presence of the speaker in person was more effective than recordings (audio). This would appear to be true for second-language speakers, since live speakers, even when delivering a prepared presentation, at a certain level are interacting with the audience, and subconsciously monitoring the audience's reactions, and intuitively making adjustments. What is more, the technical quality of many video and audio recordings is poor, again placing unnatural demands on students.

None of the above, however, is intended to suggest that there is no place for audio and video recordings in the classroom. By using recorded material, it is possible to bring the whole world into the classroom, including other dialects. Also, dialogue and group discussion can be presented to students through recordings. In fact, what I am suggesting is that both live and recorded material be used in the course.

4.8. Attitude and Motivation Should Be Considered

It is my belief that motivation is of paramount importance in any good teaching, and certainly in teaching ESL. Students who are not motivated, or are irritated with the activities or the approach, or fail to see how they will benefit them, will not learn well.

Naiman et al. (1978:66), in their "Good Language Learner" study, confirm, as do earlier findings (Gardner and Smythe 1975), that attitude and motivation, in many instances, are "the best overall predictors of success in second-language learning." However, they are careful to clarify that attitude and motivation may be necessary conditions, but are not sufficient conditions for success in learning a second language.

The implications of the importance of motivation are enormous when planning a listening course: The material and tasks and activities must be motivating. And I would argue that the material will be motivating when it is pitched at the right level, interesting for students at their particular age and intellectual stage, deemed to be relevant to their experience, and judged to be contributing to their language learning needs. I believe that a strategy-based program can and should meet all these requirements.

Coupled with this, students will be motivated when they need to communicate, for example, to complete a task or to solve a problem. This should be reflected in the types of activities developed, for example, "information gap" and "jigsaw" activities (see Section 10.3). Ur (1984) adds to the above by arguing that motivation and interest can be increased by making active responses to what is being listened to rather than by listening passively. She goes on to suggest that if something is fun, this too will be a motivating factor. In the same vein, Oxford, Lavine, and Crookall (1989) call for "simulation/gaming." While one tends to associate simulations and games with the productive skills, particularly with speaking, there is certainly a place for these in listening as well.

4.9. Listening Courses Should Account for Different Types of Listening

Often listening courses fail to address the issue that there are different types of listening, and that good listeners listen to different things in different ways, precisely as good readers read different things in different ways. For example, one should not listen to the news and to directions how to get to some place in the same way. The different listening passages in many courses tend to be very similar, as do the types of tasks required of the learners. This variation of types of listening and of listening tasks should be reflected in any general course material (see Chapter 9).

4.10. A Listening Course Should Recognize the Importance of Prior Knowledge

This principle is one of the cornerstones of my strategy-based approach.

Listening does not simply mean hearing and comprehending what has been said. It is a complex process of hearing what has been said *and linking it with* the learners' prior knowledge of the topic (also referred to in the literature as "world knowledge"). When we listen in a language in which we are proficient, we draw from our store of prior knowledge, subconsciously filling in information that has not been explicitly stated—we activate our existing schemata. Substantial empirical evidence exists showing the great importance and positive effect of using and building/teaching background knowledge when trying to comprehend.[10]

A listening comprehension course should be so devised that students listen to something and form a hypothesis which they can then link to prior knowledge they have stored as a schema. The schema needed has to be "activated" or "retrieved," and one of the teacher's tasks is to help students build this bridge between the "new" that they are hearing, and that which they already know. This is done through the prelistening activities described below, and it is this that makes prelistening activities in an ESL listening course so important.

This process of drawing on prior knowledge enables learners to make viable hypotheses, predictions, and inferences—in real life situations, some of our comprehension is not just through understanding what has been explicitly stated, but rather through linking it to a schema that we have stored away. Of course, as was discussed, this activation of a schema presupposes that the learner in fact *possesses* that prior knowledge, but this is not always the case, particularly when the material is very heavily "culture-bound"—i.e., culture-specific. The question of what we as teachers of listening should do when learners do not possess the necessary schema, is addressed below. However, what is very clear from the research is that background knowledge is extremely important for comprehension, and when it is lacking, it must be taught.

4.11. Prelistening Should Precede the Listening

Nichols (1955), writing about teaching listening to native speakers, emphasizes that "we must give prior thought to the topic. One of the best known ways to stir up interest in a topic is to discuss it with our friends before hearing the formal presentation of it" (p. 295). When listening in our first language in the real world, it is the norm that we know something about what we are listening to, and only in the exceptional cases that we do not. An example would be switching on the radio or television in order to hear the news, and to hear it introduced by the words, "Here is the news . . ." An example to the contrary would be if we just switched on the radio or television out of boredom and began listening to whatever was being broadcast. This kind of listening task, if

---

[10] For evidence of the importance of background knowledge, see Steffensen, Joag-dev, and Anderson (1979); Mueller (1980); Stevens (1982); Alderson and Urquhart (1985); Lee (1986); Floyd and Carrell (1987)

we needed to listen closely, would be dramatically more difficult than if we have given some prior thought to the topic.

For second-language learners, there is even more at stake than merely "stirring up interest"—prelistening activities help ESL learners narrow down the possibilities of what it is they are going to be listening to, and help them in the vital strategies of hypothesis formation, predicting, and inferencing—also essential features of a strategy-based approach (see Chapter 8). When a piece of listening is prepared with prelistening, then already the vital first step has been taken to ensure that this is teaching and not testing.

What occurs as a result of prelistening activities such as a discussion of the general topic, is that students activate, build on, and pool their prior knowledge. This enables them to make the link between the prior knowledge that they have stored away and the new material to which they listen. This cognitive process is vital to learning in general, not only to listening. Jones et al. (1987:47) use the concept of prior experiences serving "as a lens through which to interpret." Of course, as has been pointed out, a factor that has to be taken into consideration in any multicultural class, is the amount of prior knowledge students in one class may have, and, as Dunkel (1986:103) so correctly points out, "Effective communication depends on whether the listener and speaker share a common 'semantic field.' " It is for this reason that I referred above to students *pooling* their knowledge—a means of partially compensating for lack of prior knowledge.

Prior knowledge can begin to be activated by simply looking at, or discussing the title and any visuals. Numerous suggestions exist in the literature as to types of activities that can be pursued. Of particular note is Langer's (1981) "Pre-Reading Plan," which is extremely interesting and can very successfully be adapted for listening. The prereading is in three stages. In the first stage, through discussion, the teacher judges how much prior knowledge there is on the topic. In the second stage, through appropriate questions such as, "What made you think of that?" the initial associations are extended, and the discussion also enables students to benefit from the thoughts of other students. Finally, in the third stage, students have an opportunity to modify their initial thoughts based on what they have thought of and heard in the second stage.[11]

4.12. The Students Should Know What They Will Be Listening For

When listening in the real world, we generally not only have a fairly good idea of what we are listening to before we ever begin listening, but we also have a fairly clear idea of *why* we are listening to it—of what we are going to be required to *do* with what we have heard. For example, listeners might wish to determine a specific fact, to pick up enough in order to contrast this with some other information, to get the gist of what is being said, or to answer a set of questions.

---

[11] See also Gillian Brown (1978); Gillian Brown and George Yule (1983); Richards (1983); Jones et al. (1987).

It is very common in listening comprehension classes (and in listening comprehension tests) for the teacher to have students begin the listening without having gone through the questions and/or tasks that they will be required to work on after listening. The justification for this traditionally was that going over the questions in advance might "give away" the answer—the very notion that anything is being "given away" reveals the testlike mentality that existed in what purported to be a listening lesson. Students should be aware of the questions and tasks in advance of listening because this will affect the way they approach and process the listening. In a strategy-based approach, students are trained to see that certain strategies are helpful in certain situations, or to ascertain certain things. If students do not know what they are to listen for, they cannot activate the appropriate strategies. In short, knowing the questions will make the listening more focused and therefore easier, so why deprive second-language listeners of the "help" that native speakers usually have?

4.13. Postlistening Activities Should Follow the Listening

Care should be taken in a listening comprehension course that the listening does not become an end in itself. After all, in the real world, often after listening, we *do something* with what we have listened to. For example, we may listen to directions and then act on them; we may listen to guidance as to how to fill out a form; or we may listen to a lecture and then synthesize this with our reading on the topic. In the second-language listening class, students should be required to utilize their listening in postlistening activities. What is more, this is a good opportunity to reintegrate the listening with work in other skills, for example, by having students do a piece of writing or oral reporting on what they have been listening to. (For further examples, see Snow and Perkins 1979:54; Glisan 1988:15.)

4.14. Listening Activities Should Teach, Not Test

Listening comprehension courses often take the form of a listening passage followed by a set of comprehension questions. Students are not taught how to tackle the piece of listening—they are not trained in using strategies for listening, nor are they trained to use all possible signals and cues. In other words, their listening "course" is not teaching them how to go about listening, but is, in fact, a series of *tests*—I use the term "test" advisedly, because each "lesson" is merely another opportunity to listen to a passage (precisely as in a test situation) and then answer the questions that follow. I am not suggesting that there is no value to this. What I am suggesting is that this "test-retest" approach is not the most efficient way to develop listening comprehension ability in students.

Gillian Brown (1978:280, 282–3) argues that "testing" in lieu of what I consider to be "teaching," demands "correct" answers as in tests. She concedes that there are specific listening tasks in which we can deem some response "correct," for example, if the task is to listen for very specific information. However, in longer texts, the load on memory is simply too great to demand single, correct answers. As an alternative, she proposes that in such texts as in interactive dialogue, we should "abandon the notion of a 'right' answer to a question, and be prepared to accept any answer which makes reasonable sense." This makes the very notion of "correctness" in what is heard in most rapid spoken language debatable. Clearly, we have to become much more accepting and flexible in our judgment of listeners' responses to questions.

Another problem with the testlike traditional listening tasks is that the task is almost always given at the end of the entire listening passage. This may well not parallel what actually happens in reality, and certainly places a heavy burden on memory (Joiner 1991).

4.15. The Listening Tasks Should Be Chosen Carefully

Building on what has been said above, students should have a clearly defined task or assignment or set of questions before listening. This activates the schemata and world knowledge that they possess. What is more, listening tasks should be authentic and akin to what one does with such a piece of listening in the real world. For this reason, one kind of activity that I personally oppose is having students read along while listening. I believe that this reinforces the sense that spoken English is "oral written text"—a notion that we are trying to wean them away from in a listening course. If the passage is so difficult that students need to read along, then it is probably an inappropriate passage for those students.

As Ur (1984) cautions, care must be taken to keep the design of the tasks simple, so that most of the time is spent on the listening passage itself and not on the explanation of the logistics of a complicated activity. Tasks relating to pictures and diagrams are often simple administratively, and very effective (see Ur for examples). Ur also makes the point that if the listening passage is *particularly* interesting or enjoyable, then one can even dispense with a task!

Another important principle to be followed is that there be a lot of variety in the kinds of activities. First, this will contribute to motivation—I have too often seen listening courses in which the designers have come up with a "blueprint" or "skeleton" of what a unit will contain, and used this outline in every unit. This is both monotonous and unmotivating. What is more, not every point to be taught lends itself to the same treatment or to the same kinds of activities. Also, not all responses have to be verbal, and Ur (1984) provides fine examples of responses with pictures, strip-stories, diagrams, and more.

Parallel to the call for a large number of different kinds of activities, there should be a variety of texts. Not only is it a fact that all texts are not suitable for all listening tasks, but using many texts will also increase motivation.

In keeping with his characterization of listening as an "interpretive language process," Murphy (1985) suggests that the activities should not be of the "listen to the whole text and then respond" type (he sees these as too "testlike"), but rather listeners should be stopping and starting the listening and *interacting* with it (see also Burbridge 1986). Where appropriate, students should be encouraged to negotiate meaning with the speaker: listening, according to Murphy (1985:23), is "an interpretive language process that embraces the interactive negotiation of meaning between speaker and listeners."

Finally, we must be very careful not to overburden our students with tasks and memory loads that are not realistic even for native speakers. Gillian Brown (1978) points out that if students are going to be asked to remember details from a passage, then they should be permitted to take notes in writing—if writing is not going to be permitted, then, she argues, the texts should not exceed thirty seconds in length.

For examples of types of listening activities, see Richards (1983:235); Lund's "listener function" and "listener response" taxonomy (1990); Rost (1991:124–125); and Omaggio-Hadley's tasks, which are usefully divided into "novice/intermediate" and "advanced/superior" (1993:174). Finally, for an excellent and very extensive collection of actual classroom listening activities spelled out in detail, see Ur (1984:Part 2).

4.16. Training Should Be Given in Recognizing and Interpreting the Linguistic Signals

There are signals built into the linguistic system of English which tie directly with the information structure, and which assist listeners in comprehending when listening. For example, attention to the speeding up and slowing down of what is being said ties directly with what is being stressed and given prominence and what is of lesser importance to the message. These signals provide very useful clues not only to the meaning of sentences, but also to the structure of the discourse. Another example of a linguistic signal which can help listeners is the markers in English which make the relationship between propositions explicit. If, for example, someone explains a complex point, and then begins the following utterance with, "For example . . ." then competent listeners know that what will follow will be exemplification of what has just been explained. If, on the other hand, the opening words of the utterance following the explanation are, "On the other hand . . ." then competent listeners know that what will follow will be an expression of the opposite view. Probably the most important linguistic signals of all are lexical— word identification. By linking such a word to prior knowledge, hypothesis formation and prediction are possible.

Second-language learners know *subconsciously* how systems of this type operate, from their competence in their first language. However, for learners to begin to take note of, and to utilize such features in a second language, requires that this be brought to a conscious level by means of some consciousness-raising work. Moreover, linguistic systems and signals are not universally consistent over languages and we therefore cannot assume that once the learner's consciousness has been raised, the linguistic signals will be processed correctly in English. An example of a difference across languages is the rules of stress/unstress of syllables in English, a stress-timed language, which differ markedly from the rules in syllable-timed languages such as French. As a result, native speakers of a syllable-timed language require training in how the English stress/unstress system works in tandem with the structure of information in English, in order to derive maximum benefit from this when listening to spoken English (see Section 7.2).

As will be seen in the later chapters, much of the strategy training that I am proposing is aimed at students utilizing the linguistic, extralinguistic, and paralinguistic signals to the maximum.

4.17. Attention Should Be Given to Extralinguistic and Paralinguistic Clues

In the real world, native speakers make maximum use of clues to meaning from background noise, setting, what people wear, etc., (extralinguistic features), and to loudness and softness of speech, gesture, variation in voice quality, etc., (paralinguistic features of communication).

Teaching with the audiolingual approach, the focus was on the *words* themselves. Not only were these nonlinguistic cues traditionally neglected, but they were often *deliberately* played down or "edited out." For example, in many traditional intermediate-to-advanced level listening comprehension courses, care was taken to make recordings devoid of background noise. It was argued that the background noise might distract learners, whose attention should be on the words. In addition, there was a belief that some of these extralinguistic cues would "give away" the meaning. It is precisely because I believe that this is true, and that a great deal can be learned from these clues, that I argue for their *inclusion*. What is more, I believe that a listening comprehension course for second-language learners should train learners in strategies that will enable them to gain maximum assistance from such clues (see Chapters 6, 7, and 8 for exemplification). This is what native speakers of English do, so surely second-language learners should get at least as much help! This is also one of the reasons that I advocate the use of video rather than audio recordings, because there are more of these clues available, and visual signals reduce ambiguity and increase redundancy. (See also Kellerman 1992b.)

4.18. A Listening Course Should Include Training in Hypothesis Formation, Prediction, and Inferencing

Good listeners do a lot of predicting and inferencing. I will use the term "predicting" as guessing the whole based on a part, i.e., based on partial comprehension or on having only heard a part of the whole passage. While listening to something, competent listeners make calculated guesses as to what will come next. This takes the form of a hypothesis (a prediction) that they formulate, which they then either validate as the discourse develops, or modify as they learn that their hypothesis was inaccurate. This is an on-going process, and they constantly modify and adjust the hypothesis throughout the discourse. Most listeners do this quite unconsciously in their first language, but need to be encouraged and trained to do this in their second language.

I use the term "inferencing" as defined by Willing (1987:285–286):

> [Inferencing is] discovering a solution by deriving it from what is already known. In making an inference, in principle all the required information is present, but the solution is temporarily hidden. Inferencing operates by bringing together different parts of the known, as well as present experience, to find what they yield when merged.

Inferencing has also been described as "listening between the lines," and, in fact, that is the title of an ESL listening comprehension text by Lougheed (1985), which has very clever inferencing exercises.

Carton (1966), writing in the area of learner strategies in general, notes that learners vary in their ability to make valid, rational, and reasonable inferences.

I believe that learners can improve their predicting and inferencing skills if they are trained in the use of effective strategies, and, consequently, I see such training as an essential component of a listening comprehension course (see Chapter 8).

4.19. Initial Analysis of Needs and Ability

In order to make decisions as to the design and content of the listening comprehension course, some initial analysis and assessment is necessary. This analysis will yield information that will be vital if the course is to be relevant, meaningful, and pitched at a suitable level for the students. (See Morley [1991] for an excellent description of the principles of materials development.)

4.19.1. Assessing the Students' Needs

Different students need the language for different purposes. For example, some might be bound for postsecondary education delivered in English, calling for a major unit on academic listening, while others may not. It is not an easy matter to access this information because it is not something that students will have given a lot of conscious thought to. Even if they know why they are learning English, they are unlikely to be able to verbalize how this should translate into a course. In my experience, carefully designed questionnaires and class discussion have been the most effective way of assessing students' needs. While the teacher should be flexible if the discussion goes off in an unexpected direction, he or she must have a set of *very specific* questions. I have found that general questions yield vague and unhelpful answers.

Based on the needs analysis, it becomes possible to identify what students need to be able to do in and with the language. (This issue is discussed extensively by Richards [1983:228–230] in his list of "micro-skills.")

4.19.2. Assessing the Students' Proficiency Level

The focus of this book is not testing. However, a brief section on the importance of diagnostic testing is necessary. In many programs, students are assigned to a particular class or a particular level, but the teacher is not informed, except in the most general way, what their proficiency level is. (The classroom teacher may not even be aware of what test was used to determine the students' proficiency.) What is more, this determination of the students' level might be based on assessment that might not even include a listening component. Even when the level is reported, it is seldom accompanied by detailed diagnostic data as to each student's strengths and weaknesses. Consequently, it is usually necessary for the classroom teacher to administer a diagnostic test. Although it is beyond the scope of this book to elaborate on this testing further, one word of caution must be sounded: many of the popular, commercially available listening tests do not reflect the type of listening and listening tasks being recommended in this book. In other words, such tests' results can be misleading. As a result, care must be taken not to use an instrument that measures something different from what is going to be taught.

4.19.3. Assessing the Learners' Preferred Strategies and Learning Styles

The goal of a strategy-based approach is not to force students to use any strategy that does not suit them or to alter anything when a strategy that they already use is perfectly effective. Therefore, it is necessary to analyze the strategies and learning styles of our students. Some very effective instruments may be found in the literature, and they include the following:

- Oxford's "Strategy Inventory for Language Learning (SILL): Version for Speakers of Other Languages Learning English. Version 7.0 (ESL/EFL)," (1990: 293–300). This is probably the most comprehensive analytic tool available.

- Reid's "Perceptual Learning Style Preference Questionnaire" and "Questionnaire Statements," (1987:110–111). These are good examples of how to go about ascertaining this information.

- McGroarty's "Learning Strategies Inventory," (1987) is also very useful.

Another way of getting this information is through "think aloud" interviews (see, for example, Hosenfeld 1976 and 1979; Cohen and Hosenfeld 1981; and Chamot and Kupper 1989).

4.19.4. Assessing the Learners' Level of World Knowledge

As I have reiterated in a number of places, a strategy-based approach draws on and uses world knowledge in a very pivotal way. Information as to the students' background knowledge is therefore a very important factor in planning the prelistening activities and deciding what sorts of materials would or would not be appropriate and accessible to these students. This is vital because one of the strategies that I propose is inferencing from prior knowledge. (See O'Malley, Chamot, and Kupper 1989:433–434, for some excellent examples.)

It can often happen that in an ESL class, with students from a variety of disparate cultures, some students will lack the background knowledge on which the teacher had hoped to build. This must be addressed as part of the prelistening.

Despite the importance of knowing the level of general world knowledge of the students, it must be noted that it is extremely difficult to ascertain this beyond getting a sense of their general educational background. Consequently, a more efficient approach is to begin by determining the needs and proficiency level of the students. On the basis of this, the teacher can determine the content areas to be covered. And then, information as to the learners' world knowledge on those *specific topics* can be elicited.

4.20. The Central, Organizing Pattern of a Strategy-Based Listening Course

As has been discussed, a needs analysis is vital if any program is to be made maximally relevant, and teachers should also begin by diagnosing the proficiency level of their students and determining the strategies usually used by these students. These are preparatory steps to the design of the actual listening course.

One of the key questions growing out of the approach that I am proposing is this: *What would a strategy-based listening comprehension course look like?*

To start such a course, I would propose an introductory unit on Linguistic Proficiency (see Chapter 5). Much of this unit would not be "strategy-based." It would train students to cope with the special features of spoken English such as the unique features of "fast speech." This unit would also include training in recognizing and interpreting different discourse markers—words or expressions signaling the logical relationship between propositions, or the signals that tell listeners how the discourse is organized.

The backbone of the course and its key units should be devoted to training students to use different strategies that will assist them in their listening. This will be reflected in the titles proposed below for the different units. Clearly, a listening comprehension course would also require a unit, or a number of units in which learners are given practice in listening—where the focus would no longer be on a specific strategy, but rather, learners would be expected to apply what they had learned in unguided, uncontrolled situations (see Chapter 10). This would come at the end of the course, or be done in stages, after different strategies have been practiced. It is encouraging to note that Geddes' *How to Listen* (1988), is organized more or less along the lines that I am proposing, each unit dealing with one aspect of the listening process.

An alternate way of phrasing the question as to what the course would look like would be this: *What would the table of contents of such a listening course look like?* Traditionally, listening comprehension courses are organized in terms of the content of the listening texts, i.e., the organization could be described as "situational" or "topical." In keeping with the strategy-based approach being proposed, I would suggest organizing the material not according to the content of the texts, but *according to the strategies that are being worked on.*

In addition to a preparatory unit on linguistic proficiency, and some requiring that learners apply what they have learned to do when everything is brought together, the table of contents of this kind of course would include such strategy-based units or chapters as the following:

- Learning to determine the setting (see Chapter 6)

- Learning to determine the interpersonal relationships between the speakers (See Chapter 6)

- Learning to assess the mood of the speakers (see Chapter 6)

- Learning to determine the topic (see Chapter 6)

- Learning to determine the main meaning of each utterance (see Chapter 7)

- Learning to form hypotheses, predict, and inference (see Chapter 8)

- Learning to listen to different things in different ways (see Chapter 9)

- Learning to determine the main idea (see Chapter 9)

As indicated above, much of this will be exemplified and made concrete in the remainder of the book. However, because of not relating this book to a specific group of learners with specific needs, the content of the course can only be advocated in general terms. Rubin (1988) suggests two guiding principles in choosing the strategies to be taught. An extremely valuable criterion is to select strategies that enable students to see an immediate payoff. This is very motivating and reduces learning anxiety. She also suggests that we should concentrate on those strategies that approximate real-life behaviors rather than classroom behaviors because these will contribute more to building independence beyond the classroom.

A detailed analysis of any group of learners would likely result in some modifications to the general scheme offered here. Consequently, the description and exemplification below should not be seen as a definitive design, but rather as spelling out the principles and exemplifying them.

4.21. Designing Each Unit

Having gone through the analyses described above, it should be possible to ascertain what should be included and what should not be included in the specific listening course.

The next step is to design the individual units. I would suggest that some form of each of the following be included, and, as will become clear, this list draws on what has been discussed in detail above.[12]

4.21.1. Prelistening

This causes students to activate and utilize their existing knowledge of the topic in the listening passage by activating schemata that students already possess. This will benefit them by enabling them to predict and inference. For example, if students are going to hear a discussion about organ transplants, the teacher could have a prelistening discussion on the issue of medical ethics not keeping up with medical technology in order to activate whatever knowledge learners already have on that schema. (As has been suggested, if students are found to lack the necessary background knowledge, then steps have to be taken, by pooling the group's ideas and other means, to provide some background information.)

4.21.2. Awareness and Consciousness-Raising

When advocating a strategy-based methodology, one should not take for granted that teachers are aware of the power of strategies. A large amount of time must be allowed to train teachers to use both these new strategies and this approach. Otherwise, teachers might be resistant—the approach could be perceived as being overly controlling or contrived. Rubin (1988) points out that one of the shortcomings of her study, which aimed at improving foreign language listening comprehension, was that insufficient time was given to training teachers. (Rubin also cites Wenden [1988], who emphasizes the same point.)

Students, too, are usually unaware of the power of strategies. It is not that they do not use any strategies—everyone does—but rather that they lack awareness as to what strategies they use or how they go about learning or comprehending. They lack the different types of meta-awareness described inChapter 3. Therefore, when a strategy-based approach is being used, there should be carefully planned and deliberate consciousness-raising, and the teacher should keep students informed throughout as to what the strategy is that is being taught and why. This is in keeping with my sincere belief that students should *always* be kept informed. This gives them a sense of ownership and responsibility for the learning.

---

[12] See also Nuna (1988); Underwood (1989); Richards (1990).

For example, students need to learn to understand what introductory disclaimers such as, "To be honest . . ." or "I don't mean to be unkind . . ." signal. Competent listeners will know that what will follow such disclaimers will always be negative, but softened. Students also need their consciousness raised as to how something has the illocutionary force that it does—how, in a particular context, that string of words will have the meaning that it does. For example, they need to become aware of how tone can determine the meaning of a string of words—for instance, how tone yields sarcasm; "I'm really thrilled," said with a very small fall in pitch on "thrilled" would have to be paraphrased as "Who cares!" or "So what!" whereas the same words, with a fall from high on "thrilled" would be paraphrased as "I am truly excited!"

Consciousness-raising is also necessary with regard to signals that are available to be used and strategies that would be helpful. So, through consciousness raising, students need to be convinced of the value of such strategy training. Then they need to be trained to use effective strategies for different purposes. Numerous specific examples are cited throughout the remainder of the book.

Class discussion is the best way of raising consciousness. However, a word of caution is needed: care must be taken that this does not become a "minicourse" in linguistics—students *must* be able to see the immediate relevance and value of what they are doing and use it, not just talk about it!

4.21.3. Focusing the Listening

In the stages that precede the listening, students should be made aware of what the reason is for the listening, i.e., the questions or tasks that will follow, and what they should be listening for—details, the central idea, one particular fact, etc. As was discussed in detail above, focused listening is generally much more successful than blind listening.

4.21.4. Training Activities

In the approach that I am proposing, with "how to" as the key term, the course will include in each unit, *training activities* which sometimes will not be precisely real-life listening, but will serve as a means to that end.

Let's draw an analogy from parachuting: To be able to jump out of an airplane with a parachute, and to land uninjured on the ground (the end goal), requires that the individual go through a series of training exercises. These have all sorts of supports and protections built in, but are not yet real parachuting. For example, having been trained how to land, the parachutists practice jumping from a tower wearing a safety harness to break their fall if they go wrong and are in danger of hurting themselves. I find it hard to believe that trainee parachutists would feel that this was time wasted, or time taken away from the "real thing," and I would doubt whether any parachuting school would apologize for taking their students through these stages. The same applies to learning to listen, and it is for this reason that I propose building training activities into a listening comprehension course. As was stated in Chapter 3, research has shown that training students how to listen leads to improvement in their listening ability and training students how to listen requires training them in the use of strategies for listening.

The units of a course must not be a series of tests, but rather part of a learning program, and students need to be taken through a number of training steps that will show them how to tackle a real listening passage. The training stage is, in my view, imperative even though the supports and "predigestion" that take place may cause this not to be *natural communication*. These training activities should be specifically designed to give students practice in utilizing different signals and trying different strategies. Only if we take our students through a series of training activities, with supports and protections built in, will we be teaching them *how* to listen.

What I am proposing, then, is a model in which there are units on different strategies or aspects of listening, with training activities contained in them, and that ultimately the course will move to real listening.

4.21.5. Working with Real Data

After all of the previous steps have been completed, students should be required to handle real data with all the supports removed. And, as has been discussed above, in this phase, students require a lot of practice and a lot of exposure. It is during this stage that students will apply the different things that they have learned in the training activities.

It is very important to bear in mind that arguing for a course that teaches students how to listen does not negate or reduce the need for also providing learners with a lot of exposure to listening, i.e., giving them a lot of practice in listening. As far back as 1955, Hollow, doing research in first-language listening, found that the listening performance of fifth graders correlated with the amount of television they watched—with the quantity of exposure. The point, then, is that students will clearly benefit from a course that both teaches them how to listen, and also includes a large amount of listening.

4.21.6. Doing Something with What Has Been Comprehended

The listening should be followed by some application of what has been comprehended, such as a writing or a speaking task, in an attempt to replicate the reality of what we often do with our listening (discussed above).

4.21.7. Judging Strategy Use

As the listening course progresses, teachers should work with the students and help them to judge their use of these strategies. However, as Rost (1990) points out, there is an element of guesswork in this as the teacher cannot know what the learners are thinking. He suggests that the better the teacher knows the students and can "read" their body language, the more accurate the monitoring will be. (See Rost's section titled, "Traces of Development in Listening in Non-Collaborative Discourse," 1990:137.)

The monitoring that I am proposing should yield feedback which it is hoped will ultimately lead to learners seeking opportunities to listen to similar types of passages *outside* the classroom. In this way, this feedback provides another means of consciousness-raising.

The Linguistic Proficiency Required to Be a Competent Listener

5.1. Introductory Comments

As has been stated, the focus in this book is on strategy training in a strategy-based program. However, there is a certain level of linguistic proficiency that is required in order to handle listening comprehension. It should be noted that I am using the term "linguistic proficiency" in a broad sense to include not only mastery of features of the sound system and the grammatical system at the sentence level, but also to include mastery at the discourse level—what Canale and Swain (1980) call a "competence for discourse." As Gillian Brown (1990:11–12) states, despite the correct emphasis today on top-down processing when listening, "you still need to be able to monitor the incoming acoustic signal so that you know which of your predictions is being confirmed and which is not. You do need to be able to use all the phonetic cues that a native speaker takes for granted." Exactly what a particular group of students has control of should be ascertained by means of diagnostic testing. This chapter will describe the major aspects of linguistic proficiency needed for listening comprehension that pose difficulties for second-language learners. Identification of the linguistic features and their meanings should be practiced in a unit early on in a listening comprehension course.

It should not be taken for granted that students are able to distinguish all the sound differences that exist in English, like the [i] vowel in SHIP as opposed to the [iy] vowel in SHEEP, and the [u] vowel in PULL as compared with the [uw] vowel in POOL. Distinguishing between the vowels of English is difficult for many second-language learners because of their similarity. Identifying these distinctions is very important because several vowels sound so very similar but belong to different phonemes, so that very slight phonetic variation can alter meaning completely. The same is true for changes in stress and/or intonation.

Teaching a unit on linguistic proficiency not only ensures that students have the tools that will be necessary throughout their listening, but it also gives them confidence in tackling the rest of the course. Ur (1984:35) distinguishes such listening from all the other kinds of listening that people do, calling it "listening for perception." She correctly points out that here "actual comprehension is a secondary consideration, the emphasis being on aural perception"—hence my suggestion that this be treated at the beginning of the course. In many respects, then, a unit such as this should be seen as a preparatory unit, and will contain a high proportion of "training activities," with all that this implies.

Much of a unit like this will, of necessity, contain activities such as sound or pattern discrimination (see Ur 1984, for examples). What is more, the very "training" activities that this unit will require will likely demand either that a lot of the material is presented live by the teacher or is specially recorded for this purpose if it is to sound like real speech. When traditional listening comprehension courses address these matters, the materials are usually recorded in an overly deliberate, unnatural style. If the materials are presented in language that is deliberate, slower than normal, and with exaggerated intonation contours, etc., then it will, ipso facto, conceal the very features of spoken language that I believe this unit should be addressing, such as the characteristics of "fast speech." Fast speech is the norm for spoken English, but gives second-language learners a great deal of trouble. Gillian Brown (1990:145) points out that because of the unnatural, overly deliberate (and therefore valueless) way in which sound discrimination exercises were traditionally handled, "training in coping with the phonetic signal of speech . . . almost completely disappeared in the 1980s as a feature of courses in listening comprehension. This seems a quite extraordinary case of throwing the baby out with the bath water."

5.2. Some of the Most Problematic Features of Fast Speech

As was discussed in Chapter 1, spoken English differs quite significantly from written English. And there is some variation within spoken English according to the speed and deliberateness of the delivery.

Second-language learners coming to an English-speaking country have a great deal of difficulty with comprehending the spoken language, largely because they have never been taught how to handle it, and because very often spoken English has been presented to them as a degenerate form of "correct" written English. All too often have I heard my students say things like, "I couldn't understand what he or she was saying. If only I could see it written down!" It is for this reason that in Chapter 4 I emphasized the importance of exposing the learners in their listening course to natural sounding language, spoken at normal speed.

Before beginning the detailed discussion, it is important to note the following points:

i. Much of what will be addressed in this section is related to how fast speech rules and patterns of simplification tie in with less emphasized or unstressed parts of the utterance. However, there is an inherent pedagogical danger in doing this, which the teacher must be aware of: What I will be doing, and what the teacher will be doing with the students, is to point out—to emphasize—the "de-emphasis" of certain features, and therein lies the danger!

ii.   This will not be a finite list of fast speech features, but rather a list of the most problematic ones for ESL learners.

iii. When describing changes or "distortions," we should compare these with the citation form—the "dictionary pronunciation" of the sound or pattern in question.

iv.   I have used the symbol + to indicate juncture, / to indicate no juncture, [@] to represent the centralized, unstressed schwa vowel, and ( ) to enclose segments that may be deleted in rapid speech.

5.2.1. Distortion of Word Boundaries

In rapid speech, word and syllable boundaries often do not occur in the same place as in the equivalent citation form or written form, posing a serious problem for the second-language learner:

FISH/N+CHIPS—the words "fish and" are usually pronounced without a pause before what is audible of "and," yielding a unit more perceptually parallel to "fishing" than to "fish and."

WHY+CHOOSE vs. WHI+TE/SHOES (Gillian Brown's example, 1977)—here, the two utterances are very similar and this is very difficult for the second-language learner to process.

GLADLY+MY+CROSS/I'D+BEAR—this example is taken from the old joke of the child who chooses to name her new teddy bear "Gladly," because the teddy is cross-eyed, and she had sung so many times in church, "Gladly my cross I'd bear," processing it as, "Gladly, my cross-eyed bear."

IT'S/@+LOT/@+WORK—"It's a lot of work"—This is a common phenomenon, where a word ends with a consonant and the following word begins with a vowel. (Note that the A and the vowel in OF are reduced and centralized to [@], and the consonant [v] in OF is deleted. In my experience, students handle this fairly well until there is a string of these together, and then the utterance becomes unprocessable gibberish.

5.2.2. Weak Forms

Another serious difficulty that second-language listeners have in processing spoken language is the "weak forms" the phonetic reality that vowels in unstressed position move toward, or fully to the center of the mouth to the position of the tongue for the "schwa" [@] sound. It is even hard for them to cope with schwas in citation form; for example, in the unstressed syllables of polysyllabic words, as in the first vowel in words like SELECT, MOLEST, and ARRANGE. It is even more difficult in words, when in citation, full form, the peripheral vowel is required, for example in words like TO, THEM, and A; but more often than not these monosyllabic grammatical words are unstressed, and the vowels centralize either to a schwa [@] or to a centralized allophone of the "citation vowel":

> I WAN(T)/(T)@+LEAVE —"I want to leave"

> TELL/(THE)@M+ITS/@+PIECE+F@R@+FRIDGE—"Tell them it's a piece for a fridge"

This difficulty is compounded by the fact that these weak forms occur together with other facets of fast speech—distortion of word boundaries and elision (see below), making comprehension often very difficult.

5.2.3. Elision

Gillian Brown (1990:66) defines elision as "the 'missing out' of a consonant or a vowel":

> LAS+YEAR—"last year"—the [t] is often omitted in fast speech.

> THE+NEES/@+TH@+PEOPLE (Brown's examples)—"the needs of the people"

> PCAUSE—"because"

5.2.4. Assimilation

This is a process whereby word-final sounds are not realized in their citation form, but, under the influence of the following sound, and under the time pressure of moving the articulators quickly enough, an articulation which is closer to, or the same as that of the following sound is produced in anticipation of that sound. (This is particularly common when the place of articulation is alveolar and the articulation following is farther forward or farther back in the mouth.) There can also be assimilation of voicing— a voiceless consonant may acquire some voicing under the influence of a following voiced sound, or vice versa:

> BE+A(K)/KENNEDY+AIRPORT—"be at Kennedy Airport"—the [t] in AT moves back under the influence of the following [k], and remains voiceless, yielding a sequence of [k] + [k], which itself usually blends into one sound. See "gemination" below.

> @/WHI(B)+BOARD—"a white board"—here, the [t] in "white" moves forward in the mouth to the bilabial position, and also acquires some

voicing under the influence of the following [b], which yields a sequence of [b] + [b], but again gemination occurs.

A similar process occurs *within* words, so that the point of closure of the [g] in GOOD will be farther back in the mouth than the [g] in GEESE. The reason for this is that the [g] is influenced by the following vowel, and is "pulled forward" by the front vowel [iy] in GEESE. The [u] in GOOD is, on the other hand, a back vowel, and this pulls the point of closure of the [g] back.

5.2.5. Gemination

When one word ends with a particular plosive (stop), and the next word begins with the same plosive, then these two sound are "run into" each other in rapid speech. It should be noted that the "same sound" may not be "the same" in citation form, but in rapid speech is the same as a result of assimilation:

STOP PICKING ON VAL—The [p] followed by [p] is seldom pronounced with the first of these plosives released, then closure again for the second [p], then release of the second. Instead, gemination takes place—the closure takes place for the first [p], is held for slightly longer than normal and then there is release—in total, one closure held for slightly longer than normal.

Note that the same phenomenon takes place with the *At Kennedy Airport* example above. The [t] of AT assimilates to [k], and then gemination takes place.

5.3. Intonation

There are a number of different definitions of intonation, and what it includes and does not include. For the purposes of this book, I will limit intonation to mean, "the variation in the direction of the pitch of the voice of the speaker," as per Gillian Brown's (1990:89) definition. Other features sometimes included as part of "intonation" will be covered under "primary sentence stress" and "tone-group boundaries" (Sections 5.4 and 5.5 below).

Being able to make use of the information conveyed through the intonation system is very helpful and important when trying to comprehend spoken English. Students have to be able to *perceive* the differences in intonation, and then to *know what they mean*. For example:

DID SHE SAY WE COULD BORROW THE CAR? YES. The YES can be said in a number of different ways: with a fall from a high pitch—suggests enthusiasm or delight; with a fall from a midheight—suggests "matter-of-factness"; with a fall-rise (the pitch falls and then rises, all on the YES)—suggests something like "Yes, but . . ." or "She said we could borrow it but . . ."

Intonation plays a very central part in the communication of meaning (see Benson, Greaves, and Mendelsohn 1988) despite the fact that in ESL courses it is traditionally treated as peripheral. This is truly ironic, since, as was borne out empirically by O'Malley et al. (1985), students are aware of the importance of intonation. But being aware is insufficient, and students need to be taught how to process intonational signals. Failure to do this, is depriving students of a very significant tool that native speakers use when processing spoken language. Ur (1984) states very correctly that intonation provides important grounds for making predictions, and that this should be developed in learners.

5.3.1. A Sample Activity Training Students to Extract Meaning from Intonation

Students hear the following three dialogues, all of which take place in an office. The purpose of the activity is to perceive and correctly process the utterance *She's gone to Peru* each time it is said.

Dialogue a:
A: I have to check over some accounts, but I can't find Jenny.
B: She's away till Thursday.
A: Where did she go?
B: Don't you remember the trip she won? She's gone to Peru.
A: Lucky Maria. I really envy her. I've always wanted to visit that part of the world.

Dialogue b:
C: I have to check over some accounts, but I can't find Jenny.
D: She's away till Thursday.
C   Where did she go?
D: She's gone to Peru.
C: She's gone to Peru? But I need this information today.
D: She got a last-minute, half-price trip, and I guess she forgot to call you. Maybe I can help you.

Dialogue c:
E: I have to check over some accounts, but I can't find Jenny.
F: She's away till Thursday.
E: Where did she go?
F: She's gone to Peru.
E: Of course! How could I forget the Peruvian contract!

In Dialogue (a), when B says, "She's gone to Peru," it would probably be said with a fall from a high to low pitch. This would imply excitement and that it's not something any of them do every day, and this is also reflected in A's reaction to the information.

In Dialogue (b), when D says, "She's gone to Peru," it would be said with a very similar intonation to B in the previous dialogue. However, when C says, "She's gone to Peru," this would be said with a rising intonation, and this would imply disbelief or incredulity—this is reflected in D's elaboration that follows.

In Dialogue (c), F would probably say, "She's gone to Peru" with a fall from midheight. From E's reaction, it is clear that going to Peru is something to be expected in that office, and hence F's intonation, which makes the utterance much more matter-of-fact than the way B says the same words in Dialogue (a).

These three very similar dialogues could be used for consciousness-raising and discussion of how meaning changes despite the fact that the words are identical. This could then be followed by exercises. It should be noted that I was very careful to create a *context* that invites the different intonations, and I would strongly discourage dealing with intonational differences in isolation.

5.4. Primary Sentence Stress

In every utterance, one syllable stands out as having a larger more obvious pitch movement than the rest—it has the primary sentence stress. In "unmarked" situations (when there is nothing causing this not to be the case), primary sentence stress will occur on the last content word in the utterance:

I bought a CAR

Jon wants to give you her NAME

The words CAR and NAME carry the primary sentence stress, said with a falling intonation.

Students need to be able to identify which syllable (and therefore, which word) in an utterance has the primary sentence stress, and what the implications of this are. As will be evident from the few examples below, inability to identify and then process the meaning carried by the primary sentence stress will seriously hamper listening. The primary sentence stress is what Halliday (1967) calls the "tonic" syllable, which is part of his subsystem of intonation called "tonicity."

Students need to learn that having the primary sentence stress fall on the last content word is the norm, but that there are many situations in which this is not the case as may be seen in the following dialogues:

Dialogue a:
A: I bought a CAR.
B: It's a GREAT car.

Dialogue b:
C: Jon wants to give you her NAME.
D: I thought Jon didn't KNOW her name.

In Dialogue (a), when A speaks, the primary sentence stress is on car, as per the rule for unmarked situations. However, when B responds, B will *not* place the primary sentence stress on *car* because this is now "old" or "shared" information, and primary sentence stress may only be on "new" information—hence it moves to *great*, the last item that is "new." A similar situation occurs in Dialogue (b), and in D's response, *know* will take the primary sentence stress.

Primary sentence stress may also be used for "contrastive" stress as in the following:

Dialogue c:
E: I thought you said Lee's uncle was a NURSE.
F: Lee's AUNT'S a nurse.

Dialogue d:
G: Why did Noa give her the CASH.
H: ABBY gave her the cash.

When these utterances are said with the primary sentence stress on *aunt's* in Dialogue (c) and on *Abby* in Dialogue (d), then this is said to be a "marked" form. Contrastive stress has been set up, and F's utterances would have to be paraphrased as, "It's Lee's aunt that's a nurse, not her uncle," and H's as, "It was Abby, not Noa that gave her the cash."

5.5. Tone-Group Boundaries

Information in English is structured with one primary sentence stress per unit of information. (Halliday [1967] addresses this issue, like primary sentence stress, as a subsystem of intonation, and calls it "tonality.") The ability to identify primary sentence stress also guides listeners as to how many pieces of information are present. Therefore, it is possible to say the same words with a different number of information focuses as seen in the following examples:

A. I refused the offer because I didn't TRUST them.

B. I refused the OFFER + because I didn't TRUST them.

In Example A, there is one primary sentence stress on *trust*. In Example B, however, there is a primary sentence stress on *offer* and a second one on *trust*. So, in A, there is one piece of information, while in B, there are two. The difference in meaning is that in A, the interlocutor knows that the offer was refused, and the new information is the reason. In B, the refusal of the offer is new information, as is the reason.

5.6. Stress and Rhythm

English is a stress-timed language. This means that there is an equal amount of time (at least perceptually, even if differences are identifiable by machines) between stressed syllables, regardless how many unstressed syllables (even zero) occur between them. The more unstressed syllables there are, the more these have to be speeded up. Stress and rhythm cannot, therefore, be comfortably separated in English because the rhythm is determined by the juxtaposition of stressed and unstressed syllables.

It is extremely important for listeners to be able to distinguish stress from unstress, because of the way this is tied to the structure of information in

English. Stressed syllables are described by Gillian Brown (1990:54) as being "louder, longer, more prominent in pitch and very precisely articulated." In the first edition of her book, Gillian Brown (1977:45) states that "length is the variable that most students find easiest to control; and is a reliable marker of stress."

As a general rule of thumb, the content words are stressed, and the function (grammatical) words are unstressed, so that focusing solely on the stressed words will provide listeners with a telegraphic form of the text—the essence of the message. (This idea is developed in Chapter 7, and I demonstrate how this ability to perceive stress/unstress provides listeners with an invaluable strategy for extracting the essence of the meaning of what they are listening to.)

The identification of unstress in most cases means the identification of the less important pieces of a passage in terms of its meaning. This is as important as identifying stress, because second-language speakers often make the mistake of giving equal attention to all parts of a listening passage; by concentrating on the unstressed parts as well as the stressed, they often get "left behind" and overwhelmed.

Part of the unstressed section of a passage comprises the hesitation phenomena and "empty verbal fillers"—words or expressions that are totally insignificant to the main meaning of the passage, but whose inclusion buys time for the speaker to gather his or her thoughts while not losing the floor. Although insignificant to the meaning, as much as 30% to 50% of speaking time may consist of hesitations and pauses (Richards 1983:225), making their recognition very important. Gillian Brown (1977:108, 122) categorizes these fillers as follows: "Introductory fillers" like *well, now,* and *of course,* as opposed to what she calls "common assumption fillers"—ones where everyone is expected to agree on the statement that follows, for example, "Obviously we shall do our best ..." or "There's no doubt that ..." Some of these are "nonwords" like *um, uh,* and *mmm,* and these are more easily identified as noncarriers of meaning.

Clearly, second-language learners need to be made aware of these features of spoken English and of how they relate to imparting meaning. They have to be trained that once they are able to make this distinction between stress and unstress, they *must* focus their attention on the stressed items, and on the primary sentence stresses in particular.[13]

5.7. Discourse Markers

Often, when describing the linguistic proficiency necessary for listening comprehension, the assumption is that this means the perception of individual sounds, stress, rhythm, intonation, and syntactic patterns, and that is all. However, the linguistic system also includes the structure of units larger than the sentence or the utterance—the discourse. Second-language learners need to be made aware of how discourse is structured, how the relationship *between* propositions is signaled, overtly or covertly, for example. When these signals are

---

[13] For more detailed discussion of this, see Mcnerney and Mendelsohn (1992).

overtly present as part of the linguistic system, they are called "cohesive devices" or markers of cohesion, for example, pronominalization (see Halliday and Hasan 1976). Without this "competence for discourse" (Canale and Swain's term 1980), learners will not be able to see the "wood" even if they can see the "trees." Strategies for using these markers will be described in subsequent chapters.

Another important group of discourse markers is those that "announce" or identify the text structure or genre. Examples are cue words such as "Once upon a time . . ." and "Dearly beloved, we are gathered here today . . ." (see Jones et al. 1987:10 1 1). Since it is necessary to organize knowledge in order to learn, recognition of these markers can be very helpful, because once the learner has identified the genre, then, by analogy, there is an expectation that certain features will be present and a certain sequence will be followed. Kress (1990), however, warns that genres should not be viewed as absolutes, but must be determined bearing in mind the social and cultural context.

In a longer passage, there will be "flags"—markers—showing the structure of the discourse, and listeners have to be able to understand and to use these. For example, a speaker may say something like, "To clarify . . ."— this signals that what is to come will be a restatement of something just said, offering a second chance to listeners who did not understand the first time (one of the redundancy features of spoken English), and offering the speaker who did understand an opportunity to rest. Words like "first" or "second" usually introduce the main points in academic discourse.

In addition to the types of discourse markers described above, second-language learners also have to learn to recognize "conversation management" markers. Conversation management markers are a subset of discourse markers. Contrary to the false impression given by some traditional ESL listening courses, the majority of the English that native speakers listen to is dialogue and not monologue. This immediately introduces a tension set up by two or more interlocutors wishing to speak, and the second-language learner has to learn to cope with this. What is more, listeners in a dialogue should be watching the reaction of their interlocutors and modifying what they say accordingly.

From the perspective of the listener, the task is to understand and utilize the signals, both verbal and nonverbal, that speakers send and use to manage the conversation to their advantage. Much of the signaling is paralinguistic: sitting back in one's chair signaling, "I'm finished"; deliberate leaning forward or an audible intake of air or opening of one's mouth, signaling that one wishes to speak; or other dimensions of the complex system of signaling either that a speaker is ready to give up the floor, or is unwilling to give up the floor despite pressure to do so. Interrupting and fending off interruptions are other facets of conversation management. We must also bear in mind that the person we artificially call "listener" is seldom only a listener, and "listener" becomes "speaker," backward and forward all the time in normal conversation, making this aspect of competence very important.

Finally, not all the discourse signals are given in words. For example, a very large drop in pitch, from high to very low usually signals the end of a major section.

Making full use of the discourse markers is very helpful to second-language learners, particularly since much of spoken discourse is not so tightly structured and well-organized as written discourse (Richards 1983), and thus markers such as "talking about that reminds me of . . ." become particularly important for listeners to help them to follow the thread and to make the connections. Consequently, in spontaneous speech, the role of the discourse markers is often to "compensate" for the lack of organization of the discourse, whereas in well-organized written language they tend to complement the organization.

5.8. Understanding Communicative Functions

In addition to all of the above, second-language learners have to cope with the fact that the same string of words, the same "linguistic form," can have a number of different communicative functions (different illocutionary force)—can mean a number of different things. And conversely, one particular meaning (function) can be expressed by a number of different linguistic forms. In other words, the myth, which is not uncommon in ESL courses, that there is a one-to-one correspondence between a particular linguistic form and what it can mean, has to be dispelled. For example:

IS THIS YOUR JACKET—this can mean such different things as "I'm seeking information as to whether this is your jacket" and "Please hang your jacket in the closet"—one form, two meanings or functions.

SIT DOWN; I HAVE ASKED YOU TO SIT DOWN; and WOULD YOU SIT DOWN—these can all function as commands despite the difference in form.

Students have to learn to accept this non-one-to-one equivalence, and then to be trained to interpret utterances, drawing heavily on the circumstances under which they are said—it is the variation in circumstances such as setting, atmosphere, interpersonal relations between speakers, etc., that determines what a particular utterance will stand for in a particular piece of discourse. Learning to master this is essential if one is to become a competent listener.

A listening comprehension course should include activities that train students to understand the communicative functions of different utterances in different circumstances. A very useful way to raise students' consciousness is through "paradigm activities"—training activities in which a paradigm is set up, and then one feature of the pattern is varied while the rest is held constant, so as to bring to a conscious level how meaning changes and what has caused the change. For example, students could be exposed to the same utterance, and the words would be held constant, but it would be said in different settings or by different people whose interpersonal relationships differ, and discussion could be held with students as to the meaning of the utterance each time.

5.9. Concluding Comments

It is essential to ensure that students have the linguistic proficiency required for competent listening. When this is not the case, training activities are necessary so that they can acquire this linguistic proficiency. These activities should then be linked with training activities that raise students' consciousness as to how language functions, and how to extract meaning from what they are hearing. As I have stated, a preparatory unit on linguistic proficiency for listening is advisable, and then subsequent training should be provided on additional features of the linguistic systems as needed.

Strategies to Determine Setting, Interpersonal Relationships, Mood, and Topic (SIMT)

6.1. Introductory Comments

When listening, there are six key questions that should be asked that will facilitate comprehension: *where, when, who, how, what,* and *why.* These six questions provide essential information to listeners in the following areas:

WHERE and WHEN something is taking place relate to the setting.

WHO the speakers are relates to the *interpersonal relationship* between the speakers.

HOW, i.e., the tone in which things are being said, relates to the *mood* or *atmosphere.*

WHAT is being talked about and WHY, i.e., the circumstances surrounding what is being said, relate to the *topic.*

In this chapter, I will suggest strategies that assist students in determining setting, interpersonal relationships, mood, and topic (SIMT). It should be noted that successfully determining any one of these parameters does not necessarily tell students enough to facilitate full comprehension. Even establishing the topic still does not tell listeners exactly what is being said. However, successfully determining any one of these parameters does dramatically narrow down the possibilities, and greatly enhances the chances of successful predicting, hypothesis formation, and inferencing. For example, identifying that a conversation is about marriage, and/or that it is taking place in an office between a minister of religion and a man and woman who are holding hands, and/or identifying that the mood is friendly and "loving," and then linking this to the learners' world knowledge, goes a long way toward comprehension. Based on the maximal utilization of these signals, learners are urged to guess the total meaning.

Much of "SIMT" can be had by making use of the identifiable signals, both inside and outside of the linguistic system itself—through linguistic, paralinguistic, and extralinguistic signals.

6.1.1. Linguistic Signals

These are reliable features within one of the linguistic systems (syntax, lexis, morphology, phonology, etc.) that can be used to get at some aspect of meaning. For example, when discussing strategies to determine topic in Section 6.5, I will argue that lexical signals are the most important. Another feature that is of enormous value in determining the essence of the meaning of an utterance is being able to identify stress as opposed to unstress, and to know how the stress/unstress system links with meaning structure in English (see Chapter 7). Gillian Brown (1977 and 1990) also places a lot of importance on such linguistic signals as jaw opening and lip rounding as keys to what segment is being produced. I personally have not found that those sorts of linguistic clues to the segment being produced are very helpful to average, linguistically naive second-language learners.

6.1.2. Paralinguistic Signals

These are the aspects of oral communication that lie just outside the linguistic system as it is traditionally defined, but are vital to both the production and comprehension of spoken English. They include body language, gesture, facial expression, pausing, speed of speech, loudness and softness, conscious variation in voice quality, and more (see Noller 1984). They are features defined by Gillian Brown (1990:112) as "those which contribute to the expression of attitude by a speaker."

Many different paralinguistic signals will be discussed and emphasized throughout this chapter. It is encouraging to note that O'Malley et al. (1985:43) found in their study that second-language learners "seemed aware of the importance of paralinguistic factors" (see also Kellerman 1992b). The finding of O'Malley et al. is very important since much of the strategy training I am proposing below, builds on this very assumption. It should also be noted that in my discussion of different strategies to determine different aspects of meaning, I will be talking about certain paralinguistic features as if they were functioning independently. This is, of course, not what actually occurs, and their isolation is strictly to emphasize that feature. In reality, as Gillian Brown (1977:126) states, we should be thinking in terms of "bundles of some of these [paralinguistic] features."

6.1.3. Extralinguistic Signals

These are factors that are clearly outside of the linguistic and paralinguistic systems, but are still essential for total comprehension. They include such things as background noise, visual signals making it possible to identify where something is taking place, and choice of clothes being worn. Ur (1984:5) feels that although noises, smells, and other sense stimuli do contribute background information, "most environmental clues [extralinguistic signals] are visual." This claim is very important when arguing the case for using video—and not audio-recorded material in the listening class.

This utilization of paralinguistic and extralinguistic signals in second-language listening is not so much a matter of teaching second-language learners new strategies. It is more a question of causing learners to *transfer* what they do quite naturally in their first language into the second language. This does, of course, raise the question of how universal these signals are. Popular opinion among second-language teachers is that the cultural differences are enormous—a notion which I believe to be false. Many of the manifestations of mood and attitude of speakers tend to exist in most cultures, and are therefore readily identifiable to learners even if there are minor differences, for example, of degree. Examples are nervousness, anger, desperation, excitement, enthusiasm, sincerity, authority, and emphasis (Gillian Brown 1990:137). Having students look for signals that function in the same way in English as in their first language will help the students gain confidence in general "signal use." As Kellerman (1992b) points out, many of these signals cross language and cultural boundaries when they occur *in conjunction* with words, i.e., to support or underscore the words. Those signals which tend to be culture-specific or language-specific are those which function independently of words, such as the "thumbs up" sign—what Ekman and Friesen (1969) call "emblems."

Students have to develop a conscious awareness of the importance of these signals before launching into a series of activities that will train them in their strategic use. Simply telling them that it will help is unlikely to convince them. Instead, activities can be developed in which students hear sets of texts, with and without the signals they could be utilizing. For example, they could hear the same piece of difficult text with and without helpful background noise (say, mournful organ music), and a discussion could be held as to how the background music helped limit the possible meanings, and led to a correct hypothesis. These consciousness-raising discussions should be held with students throughout their strategy training. They should involve discussion as to how, for example, students knew or comprehended something or identified what they were listening to.

An additional point that has to be brought to the attention of learners throughout strategy training of the type that I am proposing is that using these strategies sometimes leads the listener astray. For example, there may indeed be soft, mournful organ music in the background, but the text may be a conversation about a baseball game or a drinking spree in a bar, and not about what we might have predicted given the organ music. In fact, as is discussed later, not only do we need to train students to use these signals, but we also need to expose them to situations in which the signals do not help and in fact lead listeners in the wrong direction. In spite of the potential pitfalls, these strategies are more often than not very helpful and reliable.

6.2. Setting

It is very helpful for listeners who cannot comprehend everything to which they are listening to be able to establish the setting—where something is taking place (and, if it is, for example, a piece of drama, when it is taking place as well). The reason for this is that more often than not, knowing the setting suggests what the topic might be. For example, if the setting is a men's locker room, there is a good chance that the passage will be about sports.

Setting can often be had by using extralinguistic signals. The physical surrounds, background noise, clothes people are wearing, etc., help a great deal in comprehending spoken English. It is ironic that in traditional listening comprehension courses, not only are extralinguistic and paralinguistic signals not utilized, but, as I pointed out above, using them is viewed in some perverse way as "giving away" the answer. If, indeed, these signals "give away" the answer, then we should be capitalizing on them, and *encouraging* our students to utilize them. We should not be carefully editing them out of listening comprehension course materials. If we do, and thereby cause our students to rely solely on the words they hear, we are giving our second-language learners a more difficult task than that of the native speakers, who use all these nonword signals. What is more, we are inadvertently teaching our students bad habits—to concentrate entirely on words and to ignore all else.

There is a linguistic feature that also contributes to determining setting, and that is the fact that certain formulaic utterances and idioms are usually linked to certain settings. For example, just grasping the expression, "Not guilty," is sufficient to hypothesize that the setting is a trial. And, knowing that, leads to all sorts of predictions and even inferences. The very simple question, "Who's got the answer to number five?" tells competent listeners that the listening probably takes place in some sort of classroom. (As I have stated throughout, this may not in fact turn out to be correct, but usually it will be.) This point becomes very clear if we compare what we can learn and predict from hearing: "He struck him" as opposed to hearing, "He struck him out." So, by identifying these "formulas," learners can identify the setting, and this will help them to narrow down the possibilities as to what they are listening to. This, in turn, will help them fine-tune their expectations as to what they will hear. Sometimes a certain syntactic form is identified with a certain setting or speech event. For example, the use of the simple present tense identifies the following as a live commentary: "He shoots but it hits the post."

Before beginning to discuss activities and strategies to determine the different aspects of SIMT, it is important to reiterate that none of these parameters of SIMT function independently, and I have only separated them out for purposes of emphasis and consciousness-raising. In reality, they work together, and learners should use all of the available signals together.

6.2.1. Strategies to Determine Setting

A useful way to get into the use and value of these signals is to play a game with students in which they are asked to match sound and/or visuals with certain utterances, thereby reinforcing the notion of the predictive power of knowing the setting. For example, they see a scene in a classroom, two sweaty people in a locker room, and two people sitting in a car. Then they hear, "Your squash has really improved," then, "Today, we are going to examine the causes of the French Revolution of 1789," and "Please drive carefully, and follow my instructions as you drive." These would then have to be matched with the visuals.

Students need to be encouraged at all times to pay attention to the setting—to gather clues by noticing what people are wearing, what kind of a building the talk is taking place in, what nonverbal sounds can be heard, etc. Attention to such detail can be developed, for example, by discussing this and then showing students a movie in English, followed by a quiz on these sorts of details. Students have to be discouraged in their second-language listening from trying so hard to understand every word of the verbal message that they miss these other extremely valuable clues. This is a fun activity, and at the same time heightens their awareness.

Another suggestion is to develop activities in which there is only background noise and no words or only visuals with or without background noise, but no words, for example, by showing a video with the sound turned off. Students are asked to say what they think is going on, and to explain how they arrived at their hypothesis. This could be followed by a discussion in which students are asked to suggest other signals that would be useful. This is very similar to the overall consciousness-raising activity using a totally incomprehensible language, described earlier.

6.3. Interpersonal Relationships

Interpersonal relationships include determining who the speakers are, what level of formality exists between them, and how they feel toward one another. This includes what is often referred to as "register." Listeners attempting to comprehend what is going on will be greatly helped if they are able to determine, for example, that what they are hearing is discussion between two people whose relationship is quite formal. There are paralinguistic and linguistic signals that cast light on this.

Some examples of paralinguistic signals would be the way people look at each other, how close they stand to their interlocutors, whether or not there is any touching, features of voice quality, and amount of smiling.

Linguistic signals include first and foremost, the recognition of appelatives, i.e., specific terms that one person calls another by, for example, *Sir, Your Honor, Snookums, Dr. Sloman*, and *Professor Higgins*. These appelatives are not always present, but when they are, they are very helpful. Appelatives such as *Your*

Honor and *Doctor* can even tell listeners what the setting, and therefore the topic, is likely to be.

The syntactic style (register) chosen also reveals a great deal about the interpersonal relationships that exist. For example, the more casual (or even intimate) the relationship between speakers, the more ellipsis (omission of parts) in the utterance. Compare, for example these two responses to the question, "How's she feeling?"

"Lousy."
"She's really not feeling too good."

The form of the former signals greater informality or closer relationship between the speakers than the latter.

Formality is also often marked by a higher degree of tentativeness, and a lower degree of directness which yields a greater use of modal auxiliaries. For example, compare the more formal, "I think I would have approached it differently" with the less formal, "I would have approached it differently" or even, "Your approach was wrong." This phenomenon is particularly evident in requests (see example below).

6.3.1. Strategies to Determine Interpersonal Relationships

Before getting to the relationship between the speakers, listeners need to be able to determine who the speakers are. Gillian Brown (1990:137) very wisely suggests that students begin by identifying very basic features: Male or female? Child or adult? Young or old? Students can then move on to the following: Are they speaking in a hurry or with plenty of time? Who is speaking with authority, and who is speaking submissively? Who is speaking aggressively, and who kindly? Who is the main speaker (if there is one in this piece of discourse)? Training activities should be developed that concentrate on these features, and, as with all the training activities I suggest, the activity should include consciousness-raising discussion as to how the learners arrived at their conclusions and what signals they used.

A very simple training activity proven to be very effective in determining the interpersonal relationship between people is one in which students hear pairs or sets of similar utterances, the only difference between them being the interpersonal relationship, and students are asked what the relationship is between the speakers (derived from a suggestion in Snow and Perkins 1979). For example, students would hear sets of utterances like these:

Professor Slavens, I hope I'm not disturbing you. I was wondering if you could help me for a moment.

Professor Slavens, could you help me for a moment, please.

James, could you help me for a moment, please.

Jimmy, come over here. I need your help.

Jo-Jo. [I] need you.

An alternative way to approach register and formality-awareness is to have students listen to pairs of dialogues, and to be told what the interpersonal relationships are, and then to ask them what they notice about the grammar. For example, they might hear examples like dialogues (a) and (b) below. They would be told that the relationship between speakers A and B in Dialogue (a) is more formal than between C and D in Dialogue (b).

Dialogue a:
A: It would help if you gave her an extra iron tablet every day.
B: I don't really want to give her those. Is it really necessary?
A: Yes, I am afraid that it is.

Dialogue b:
C: Give her an extra iron tablet every day.
D: Must I?
C: 'Fraid so.

This activity would be working toward the idea that students should listen to the completeness of the grammar, as the more complete it is, the more formal the relationship is likely to be. Hopefully they would identify that Dialogue (a), the more formal one, has much more "complete" grammar than Dialogue (b).

A simple activity to emphasize the power of appelatives and the expectations they set up would be to list some of the most identifiable appelatives, and to teach them (as it is likely that many second-language learners will not know many of them) and then to have students try to guess the meanings of short utterances where the appelative is the most telling feature. For example, they might hear utterances such as the following:

a. Father, something has gone very wrong.
b. Doctor, something has gone very wrong.
c. Your Honor, something has gone very wrong.
d. Dad, something has gone very wrong.
e. Sweetie-Pie, something has gone very wrong.

It is very interesting to note how different the expectations are as to what is going to follow in each of these utterances: the first sounds like the prelude to a religious confession; the second sounds like a call for help to a doctor; the third sounds like an admission of a serious error in a court case; the fourth sounds like the prelude to a heart-to-heart talk; and the fifth is wide open, apart from the fact that the speakers are on intimate terms.

Another way to work with such data is to have students work in pairs, and their task is to suggest what the next couple of utterances would be following the one given. They would be urged to plan something that showed that they had grasped the full meaning of the first utterance with its appelative. So, the continuation of Sentence (a) could be something like, "I do not have the same feeling when I come to services as I used to." And the continuation of

Sentence (b) could be something like, "My hands don't grip things properly. I keep dropping even light things." While this example would only work with advanced-level students, similar activities could be designed at a lower level.

Building on the above, I have developed a more comprehensive activity that I call *What did they call each other?* The activity is divided into three parts: In the first part, students hear two similar dialogues, Dialogue (a) without any appelatives, and Dialogue (b) with appelatives added:

Dialogue a:
A: I'm exhausted.
B: Why?

Dialogue b:
C: I'm exhausted, Kitty-Cat.
D: Why, my Tiger?

Students discuss what more they can learn from the addition of the appelatives in Dialogue (b). In Dialogue (a), the absence of a signal to indicate the interpersonal relationship between the speakers makes the possibilities almost infinite. In Dialogue (b), while there is still insufficient data to make a precise prediction, the presence of "Kitty-Cat" and "Tiger" leads the listener to envisage certain limited possibilities as to what will follow.

In the second part, they hear a series of similar dialogues, all using the "Kitty-Cat/Tiger" appelatives, but some go on with thoroughly inappropriate language for this level of intimacy, while others are appropriate. Students are given the following instruction: *As you listen, try to decide which of the responses you expected to hear, which surprised you, and why.* The discussion would include how and why some of the dialogues evoke laughter. The following are two examples of such dialogues:

Dialogue c:
E: I'm exhausted, Kitty-Cat.
F: Why, my Tiger?
E: 'Coz your Tiger's been a busy Tiger.
F: Poor old Tiger!

Dialogue d:
G: I am exhausted, Kitty-Cat.
H Why, my Tiger?
G: I am exhausted because my heavy responsibilities weigh me down.
H: I really think it is commendable how you handle your burden, Tiger.
G: It is extremely kind of you to say so, Kitty-Cat.

In the third part of the activity, students hear short dialogues and are asked to say what the relationship is between the speakers and what is going on.

They are told to *listen carefully to what the speakers call each other*. The following are examples of two such dialogues:

Dialogue e:
I: Where did she get it from?
J: She took it from a library, Your Honor.

Dialogue f:
K: Where did she get it from?
L: She took it from a government report, Professor Willurby.

6.4. Mood and Atmosphere

When considering the mood or atmosphere of something we listen to, what we are referring to is the way one person is speaking to another at a *particular moment*. The people can be close friends, relatives, boss and employee, or have any other interpersonal relationship, but over and above that feature is the atmosphere or mood of the moment. The mood might be one of joking, arguing, showing anger, sharing a secret, emotional closeness, or several others.

Mood and atmosphere can be determined by concentrating on paralinguistic signals and the linguistic signal of intonation.

The paralinguistic signals that give clues as to mood include such things as body language and gesture, facial expression, voice quality, variation in the speed of speech, variation in pitch range, and loudness and softness of voice. For example, saying the words, "I'll be there" with a quieter, whispery voice suggests intimacy, a secret tryst, or the like. The words, "Don't ever do that again" can be said in a fairly normal, unmarked way, then loudly, which expresses anger, and then very pedantically and very quietly, which often conveys *extreme* anger.

Intonation is a very powerful meaning-carrier in English. Examples of the power of intonation are the way meaning changes when an utterance like, "I'm really happy for you," is said with a high fall, signaling enthusiasm and/or excitement, and then the same utterance is said with a low fall signaling disinterest, disdain or sarcasm. Similarly, consider an utterance like, "Don't cry," said with different intonations—its illocutionary force can change from an order (high fall) to a paternalistic attempt at calming the individual down (low rise).

Recognizing the importance of intonation does not mean that the words themselves are unimportant. The question then arises as to what happens when there is a mismatch between the words and the paralinguistics. This is illustrated by the old story told of the hotel guest who greets the reception clerk very warmly, and the clerk, who looks like thunder, replies, "Good morning." When asked if everything is okay, she barks back, "Everything's fine!" At this point the hotel guest says, "If that's the case, please tell your face." It has been proven over and over that in such cases, the "truth" will probably lie with the paralinguistics not with the words (Lyons 1972).

6.4.1. Strategies to Determine Mood and Atmosphere

As with setting and interpersonal relationships, much can be learned about mood and atmosphere from watching videos with the sound turned off. Students can be trained to watch for different visible features, and many of these, such as visual signs of anger, happiness, and sadness, cross cultural boundaries and are the same in the learners' home cultures. Audible features can be listened for if a foreign film is shown—however, care must be taken that the sections used do not contain examples of cross-cultural differences.

As was stated above, intonation, in conjunction with paralinguistic signals, tells a great deal about mood, atmosphere, and attitude. Degrees of enthusiasm need to be discernible to learners and they need to be trained to listen, for example, to how high-pitched an utterance is since this is a very good measure of enthusiasm—the higher the pitch, the greater the enthusiasm. Tapes can be made that train students to listen for, and to interpret this. These should include really low-pitch responses which would be classified as unenthusiastic, even if the words seemed positive: "That's good." Very simple activities can be used for this, like having students listen to little dialogues and note on a chart the degree of enthusiasm shown in each response.

Students can listen to tapes in which the same words are repeated with different voice qualities, and predict what will follow. For example, the words could be as simple as, "There's someone coming down the hall." This could be recorded with a "whispery voice," suggesting something conspiratorial; high-pitched, suggesting excitement and enthusiasm; shouted out, suggesting panic or fear; and so on. The same thing could then be done with video tape, which would add the dimension of facial expression and visual clues.

Another type of activity that is very useful in making students more aware of these signals and their importance is where students hear the same exact words in a dialogue twice, the only difference being that the first time they hear the dialogue, it is all said in "normal" voice, and the second time, the first speaker uses a "whispery voice" for the last part. An example of a dialogue that could be used would be the following:

A: Jane, have you met the new office secretary yet?
B: No, not yet. Why?
A: She's really nice. Did you know that she's pregnant?

After listening to the dialogue in normal voice, students would discuss what information they gained from it. Presumably they would say that they learned that A and B seem to work together, probably are equals, and that A is telling B in a very matter-of-fact way that the new secretary is pregnant. Then the recording with A using "whispery voice" would be played, and a similar discussion held. This time, a great deal more information is learned from precisely the same words. In addition to all that was learned from the first recording, this time there is clearly something secret about the fact that the secretary is pregnant, and A is confiding in B. This would also suggest that their superiors and others do not/should not know about this. It might also imply that the relationship between A and B is quite close. This kind of activity could be followed by a "prediction activity" in which students would be asked to guess (predict) what might follow the dialogue said in the two different ways.

Special care must be taken to recognize sarcasm—something that is very often lost on second-language learners (as was discussed in Section 4.21). They have to realize that sometimes words in English are deliberately used with the intention of them having the exact opposite meaning to what they normally have. For example, the expression, "That's great" in its "unmarked form," would be a strong expression of enthusiasm. However, said with appropriate sarcasm conveyed through voice and facial expression, it could mean just the opposite:

C: Alex's back in town.
D: [low pitch] That's great.

They would then be asked to predict what C might say next. I would expect something like, "I'm not very pleased about it, either."

6.5. Topic

Of the four SIMT components, I have deliberately chosen to deal with "topic" last. This is because everything that can be learned from identifying the setting, interpersonal relationships, and mood feeds into the topic, and contributes to the listeners' comprehension. Moreover, knowing the topic is the most important of the four parameters of SIMT for predicting, inferencing, and hypothesis formation as to total meaning. Therefore, when we consider how learners determine topic, we see that it is by linking everything that they have gleaned about setting, interpersonal relationships, and mood to their world knowledge—the schema that they already possess.

It is important to emphasize that there is one signal, quite apart from all that has been discussed so far in this chapter, that is of paramount importance in determining topic, and that is the lexical signal. If listeners are able to understand just two or three key lexical items from something they are listening to, they will probably be able to work out what the topic is, and from that, with the help of the "SIM" of SIMT, they will be able to guess the entire meaning. These couple of words (so much the better if more are identifiable) will usually enable listeners to work out the semantic (lexical) field (also known as the "universe of discourse"), i.e., the topic. For example, identifying the words "riots" and "unemployment" will suggest to listeners that they are listening to something about riots, probably due to unemployment. This immediately calls up the listeners' world knowledge of this topic, and this in turn enables them to predict much of what is going to be said. What is more, merely grasping these two words drastically narrows down what the total meaning could be.

This strategy is very powerful, and by using it judiciously, much can be understood with very little language. Therefore, language teachers must encourage their students not to give up, even when what they are listening to seems at first to be much too difficult for them. This immediately raises the question of what happens when *no* words that identify the semantic field are known. This will be addressed below.

6.5.1. Strategies to Determine Topic

"Guessing games" have proven to be very useful training in identifying topic through semantic field.

Students are given a couple of words and then asked what they know about the topic, and what they think they are going to hear. This is followed by a difficult listening task on that topic, and a discussion as to whether they were correct, how they had to modify their hypotheses, etc.

Another technique that I have used both to convince students of the power of this semantic field strategy and to help them when they really cannot identify even two or three words, is to *teach* two or three key words from the text, and then go through the same guessing procedure. It is remarkable how the same students who were convinced on first hearing the passage that they could not understand anything, can now manage quite well.

The above only works if students have a preexisting schema to activate. Due particularly to cross-cultural differences, this may not be the case. When this situation occurs, it is important that the prelistening makes some background knowledge available either from other students in the class or from the teacher. However, care must be taken that this is done with the utmost sensitivity, particularly if some members of the class have the background knowledge and others do not. The absence of a helpful schema is likely to be as a result of cultural differences and those learners must not be made to feel "stupid."

Another strategy directly related to determining topic is determining the "overall theme" (Cohen's term 1990) or main idea of a passage. A strategy Cohen advocates for getting at this is listening only for the main idea without worrying about details. Early on in their training, learners can be trained to do this by being exposed to one or two minutes of conversation between native speakers, i.e., "eavesdropping" on natural language, and making an effort to understand the message at least globally (Cohen, drawn from the work of Stevick 1984).

Rubin's (1988) "cognate strategy" is also helpful: students are encouraged to listen for cognate words from their first language. For example, many languages have borrowed English words like *terrorism, supermarket, ambulance,* and many more into their language, and ability to identify these is very helpful in determining topic. In a parallel manner, students could be trained to listen for proper names that they recognize. This strategy is particularly helpful when listening to such "universals" as the news.

6.6. What to Do About Mismatches

Throughout this chapter, I have made mention of the fact that all of the SIMT signals can lead listeners to make wrong guesses as to the meaning: not all talk in a house of worship is related to religion, and not all talk about philosophy takes place in a university. It is essential to keep on reminding students that mismatches occur all the time (although an examination of traditional listening materials would not support this).

To destroy the myth that there can be no mismatches, and to train students how to cope when these mismatches occur, activities should be developed for use *after* the "predictable" ones described above. In these, there should be a deliberate mismatch between one or more of the SIMT signals and the real meaning. It is at this point that the notion of "hypothesis formation–hypothesis modification" can be introduced (developed in detail in Chapter 8). For example, students could listen to a passage that takes place in a sports stadium, and be asked to predict what they are going to hear. They would then hear a discussion about religion, despite the location. They would, of course, have to modify their hypotheses. In real life, particularly when we come in on the middle of a conversation, we have to modify our hypotheses a number of times, and sometimes we are wrong all the way. What our students stand to learn from this is that making a wrong hypothesis is normal, and they should not get upset when it happens.

6.7. Bringing All the SIMT Training Together

After having done all the training to develop strategies to identify the different aspects of SIMT separately, it is necessary to bring all this together. This should be done by developing activities that deliberately do this. For example, students could be asked to watch short dialogues on video like (a), (b), and (c) below, after each of which, they would be required to fill out a chart like the one also shown below.

Dialogue a:
A   Gee! More cuts coming!
B: Oh no! Who gets the chop this time?
A: [whispering] Greg.

Dialogue b:
C: Vanessa, would you please type this up and make ten copies. I
     need it for this afternoon.
D: Sure, Andy. It'll be ready long before then.

Dialogue c:
E: What a party!
F: Alan and Linda have done it again.
E: Uh-huh.

The following is an example of a chart that students could be asked to fill in for each dialogue:

SETTING

Where is this happening? _____

How did you decide? _____

INTERPERSONAL RELATIONSHIPS

What is the relationship between the speakers? _____

How did you decide? _____

MOOD

What is the mood? _____

How did you decide? _____

TOPIC

What are they talking about? _____

How did you decide? _____

6.8. Concluding Comments

Having done all of the above, it is necessary to provide learners with a lot of practice in applying these strategies to real language data. I have found in my teaching that one of the most useful ways of doing this is by having students listen to conversations from the middle, and then having them try to determine different aspects of what they are listening to using the strategies they have been practicing.

7

Strategies to Determine the Main Meaning of an Utterance

7.1. Introductory Comments

This chapter will focus on the individual utterance. I will suggest different strategies, by means of which learners will be able to get at the *essence* of the meaning of the utterance. The strategies that are recommended may not yield the *exact* and *total* message contained in the utterance, but they will help to determine its main idea. I will suggest different strategies for getting at the essence of the meaning by focusing on the stress/unstress system in English, primary sentence stress, existing schemata and world knowledge, and discourse markers.

7.2. The Stress/Unstress System

One of the things that competent listeners have to be able to do is to judge what is an important information-carrying item, and what is not. Second-language listeners have to be trained to listen for the signals that identify an item as an important information carrier, and then to apply this in such a way as to grasp the essence of the meaning of the utterance. In this section, I will show that the key to identifying the high-information items in English is the stress/unstress system.

In Section 5.6 I explained the importance of learners being able to identify stress and unstress when listening in English. It is my contention that listeners who can identify that which is stressed and that which is unstressed will have come a long way toward getting at the meaning of an utterance. As Gillian Brown (1990:151) argues, the stressed words "mark the richest information bearing units." Making use of these rich phonological cues will pave the way for the top-down, inference-driven interpretation which we are striving toward.

Second-language learners (and sometimes even people training to be teachers of ESL) often fail to grasp the enormous value in being able to identify stress. Stress usually occurs on the main meaning-carrying words in an utterance. The meaning-carrying words are usually the *lexical words* ("the words that carry the meaning of the utterance—nouns, main verbs, adjectives and adverbs" [Gillian Brown 1977:49]), and identifying these lexical words usually leads listeners to the essential meaning of an utterance. The *grammatical words* ("words that show the relations between the parts of an utterance—conjunctions, prepositions, pronouns and so on" [Gillian Brown 1977:49]), on the other hand, are usually unstressed, and are usually not needed in order to determine the essence of the meaning:

> There is a **GROWING NUMBER** of **STUDENTS** that are **COMPETING** for the **DWINDLING SPACES** in our **UNDERFUNDED SCHOOLS**. [words that are stressed are capitalized]

If we string together the stressed words and delete the unstressed words, this yields the following:

> GROWING NUMBER STUDENTS COMPETING DWINDLING SPACES UNDERFUNDED SCHOOLS

The meaning of the utterance is still clear.

Students have to learn to focus on the lexical words. The strategy that I am proposing, is based on the following logic:

Teach students to understand the difference between *grammatical words* and *lexical words*. Then train students to identify the auditory qualities of stress—identifying that which is stressed usually means identifying the lexical words. Finally, putting together the stressed words yields a telegraphic version of the message, i.e., the essence of the message.

A by-product of using this strategy is that listeners learn not to pay major attention to unstressed items, thereby learning not to concentrate with the same intensity on every word. This not only focuses their attention, but increases the likelihood that they will be able to keep up with listening to speech delivered at normal speed. As well, the unstressed sections will also contain the empty verbal fillers like "you see" and "well," which the native speaker knows to process as nothing more than a hesitation phenomenon, but which often throws non-native speakers.

The following are some examples. The words that are stressed are capitalized.

> My UNCLE who WORKS in TAIWAN KNOWS a lot of HINDI.

> You should BRING JON'S TEST to them IMMEDIATELY.

> The MOTHER BEAR and the FATHER BEAR SMILED PROUDLY.

In each of the three examples, linking together the words with stress and omitting the others yields a telegraphic but comprehensible message although some of the detail is lost (see, for example, the loss of "my" in the first example and the loss of "to them" in the second).

It should be borne in mind that despite the "unmarked," most common situation described above, there are many exceptions, and sometimes the *grammatical* words are stressed, as in utterances like "PUT it *ON* the MICROWAVE [not in it]" or, "THANK *HER* for the GREAT MEAL [not me]."

The first step in utilizing this strategy of getting at the essence of an utterance by focusing on the stressed words, is learning to identify stress (and thereby, unstress). As was cited in Chapter 5, Gillian Brown (1990) describes stressed syllables in terms of their greater loudness and length, their greater pitch prominence and their greater precision of articulation. Cohen (1990:47) adds an additional acoustic feature that is helpful, and that is that key words which, by definition, are stressed, are sometimes signaled by a pause before or after them. Despite the above distinguishing features, it is not always simple to define exactly what identifies stress in every instance, but *length* is the most useful marker:

> Stressed syllables are sometimes said to be produced with more 'force' than unstressed syllables. Experiments have shown that there is no single variable always present in stressed syllables and is not present in unstressed syllables. "Force" must be interpreted in a very general way. . . . Some . . . are louder, some higher pitch, some marked by a dramatic drop in pitch, some longer. . . . Length is the variable that most students find easiest to control, and is a reliable marker of stress. (Gillian Brown 1977:45)

An additional clue to stress is through paralinguistics—head nodding, hand or foot movement, other body movement, eyebrow raising, etc., work in conjunction with the articulation.

Unstress is often identifiable by the speeding up of the production of these words, so as to maintain the stress-timed rhythm of English.[14]

7.2.1. Strategies to Determine the Essence of an Utterance

The stress/unstress system can be used to determine the essence of an utterance. However, making use of the stress/unstress system assumes that learners are being exposed to natural spoken English and not to overly slow and deliberate "teacherese." In "teacherese," not only will some of the acoustic signals of real spoken English be absent, but other distortions of real spoken English like the excessive use of stress will be present. Students should therefore be eased into listening to real spoken English as early on as possible.

One of the ways that students can be helped to identify stress is by utilizing paralinguistic signals. Gillian Brown (1990:162) advocates that students watch a film or video with the sound turned off, and try to determine when-

---

[14] For a good introductory activity that teaches this point, see Ellis and Sinclair (1989:56).

ever the speaker produces a stressed syllable: "With most native speakers this is very clearly marked by extra muscular effort of the jaw and lips or by the muscular movements of the head, eyebrows, shoulders and so on."

To make the connection between stress and meaning-carrying words, which together yield a telegraphic version of the message, a unit should be developed that takes students through a series of training activities, all of which are accompanied by consciousness-raising discussion.

The first activities would be to ensure that students grasp the relationship between "telegraphese," the essence of the message, and the full message. For this, I would work in two directions—looking at telegraphese and "completing" it by filling in the grammatical words, and creating telegraphese from a full message.

The teacher could play a game of "Newspaper Headlines" with the class, in which students are given headlines, and asked to complete them. For example, they could work on headlines such as the following:

> **POLICE OFFICER SHOT CHASING NIGHTCLUB OWNER.** (A police officer was shot while he was chasing a nightclub owner)

> **ADDITIONAL TAXES IMPOSED LAST YEAR ILLEGAL.** (The additional taxes that were imposed last year are illegal)

> **MAN MURDERED FOR GOLD CHAIN.** (A man was murdered for his gold chain)

Conversely, students could be asked to "create telegrams." A game that my students have enjoyed is one in which they are given a message, in full, and asked to prepare its content as a telegram, bearing in mind that each word is extremely expensive ($5.00). They must try to get the message across in as few words as possible. The essence of the message must be there, but as cheaply as possible. For example, they could be given messages to convert into telegrams like the following:

1. Your examination results arrived here today. You passed all of your subjects. The Calculus grade was A. Love from your Mom and Dad.

2. Your Aunt Linda had a baby girl. She is in the Park Lane Hospital. Please call your Aunt Patricia and the proud father. Love Jenny.

3. Uncle Rudolph died suddenly on Friday. The funeral will be on Monday at eleven at the village church. We are all very sad. Lee can meet you at the airport. Please call us with your flight details. Love your Mom and Dad.

The purpose of these activities is to bring students to a realization of the different functions of lexical and grammatical words, and how the grammatical words are of secondary importance in carrying information.

The next step is to link the above to stress and unstress. The teacher could begin by reading very simple sentences to the students, and asking them to identify which of the words are emphasized (stressed). For example, use sentences like these:

a BOY with a BALL was HIT by a CAR.

the PEN in your HAND is BROken.

my CAR that you adMIRE is in the garAGE for rePAIR.

Discussion should bring students to the point of recognizing that the words with the stressed syllables were said more clearly, more loudly, and more slowly and deliberately than the others. Hopefully, they would also have noticed some paralinguistic signals of stress. The goal is for them to link this to the fact that what they identified on the whole were the *lexical* words, and that if they turned these utterances into telegraphese, what they would include would be precisely these stressed words!

The next step is to train students to listen for the acoustic clues of stress in situations in which the words are *not* comprehensible to them. After all, the purpose of this training is to use this knowledge of stress and information-structure to lead them to at least a partial understanding of what they are listening to. One way of providing practice in identifying stress acoustically is by creating training activities in a nonsense language. I have developed a fictitious language that I have called "Targalian" which, I tell students, follows the stress patterns and rules of English. I have students do two types of activities. In the first, they are given a sheet with the Targalian on it, and all they are required to do is to listen to the Targalian and underline the words that have stressed syllables. For example, they would hear sentences like:

pong **FISI** vel so **KURSI** blard **GOOB** (The kitten in her garden is ill.)

WUK LASEMADA UK HIDO (Drinking causes road deaths.)

After they have become accustomed to listening to Targalian, I have them play a game in which they have to translate and complete the Targalian utterances they hear as quickly as they can. They hear utterances similar to the two above, and are supplied with a Targalian Glossary, in which *only* the stressed items are provided. The task requires students to work out the full message.

As was stated above, throughout these activities there should be discussion, and this should include discussion on the unstressed parts and what their function is. Students should be trained that the best signal of unstress is the speeding up of speech. Students should be urged to begin to listen to the stressed and unstressed parts differently, and to accept that rarely does anybody hear and understand *every single word*, and that second-language learners who try to do this will likely not be able to keep up with processing the speech they are listening to.

All of these activities are created for training purposes. They must be followed by a large amount of work identifying stress and getting at the essence of the message in real English data. Of course, as with all of the signals and strategies that I discuss, these do not in reality function in a vacuum, and should be utilized in conjunction with all the other signals and strategies that will together lead to maximum comprehension.

7.3. Primary Sentence Stress

As was described in Section 5.4, every "information unit" in English contains one stressed syllable which is produced with a larger and more obvious pitch movement than the rest—the primary sentence stress. This syllable is the focus of the information being imparted in that utterance. It is always on a syllable in a word that is imparting "new" information, never "old" or "shared" information that has already been addressed. The "unmarked" situation is when the primary sentence stress occurs on the last lexical item. When the primary sentence stress occurs anywhere else in an utterance, then this sends a very important signal to competent listeners. It tells them that the focus is not in its usual (unmarked) position, and that whatever follows this syllable will all be "old" or "shared" information. What is more, it tells competent listeners that the word with the primary sentence stress will very likely be in contrast with something else (see Section 5.4 for examples).

It is extremely helpful, therefore, for students to be able to recognize the primary sentence stress and to know what that tells them in their attempt to process what they are listening to. Of course, an additional step that is of great help to them is to identify the actual pitch movement (high-fall, low-rise, fall-rise, etc.), since this too tells a great deal about meaning (discussed in Section 5.3).

7.3.1. Strategies to Determine the Focus of an Utterance

Primary Sentence Stress is helpful to determine focus. Students have first to be trained to identify the primary sentence stress. They need to learn to identify that syllable acoustically, both by its prominence (like all stressed syllables) and its unique condition of having the largest pitch movement. Having done that, they then need to begin to work on the meaning implication of the "unmarked, occurring-at-the-end-of-the-utterance" situation versus the "marked-occurring-elsewhere" situation. Gilbert's *Clear Speech* (1984, 1993), although primarily a pronunciation text, has some very good exercises that provide practice in the identification of primary sentence stress.

An obvious type of activity is to have students listen to utterances and try to identify the primary stress. It is important that they are presented both with examples in which there is only one intonation/information unit, and others in which there is more than one intonation/information unit. In the following examples, students are given the words written out, and asked to underline the word containing the primary sentence stresses (note: with ESL students, I simply call this "the main stress").

It's a very broad **AREA.**

It's the study of **LANGUAGE,** and it's called **LINGUISTICS.**

Language has been around for as long as **PEOPLE** have been around.

Here's an example for the **SKEPTICS.**

This would be followed by a discussion of the students' answers and how they arrived at them.

A second type of activity would be to present students with the following three utterances, each with the primary sentence stress on a different word (capitalized and underlined). Students are given the numbered sentences on a sheet, all identical, and asked to underline the word with the main stress and to try to explain the meaning of the sentence:

1. Fleming discovered **PENICILLIN.** [unmarked, statement of fact]

2. **FLEMING** discovered penicillin. [marked, meaning "It was Fleming and no one else."]

3. Fleming **DISCOVERED** penicillin. [marked, meaning "He discovered it, he didn't invent it."]

This would then be practiced with more real language, and in conjunction with all the other strategies being advocated.

7.4. Intrinsic Prior Knowledge

In Chapter 6 I discussed strategies to determine topic. This should be coupled with the strategy of making maximum use of what I have called "intrinsic prior knowledge" and "extrinsic world knowledge" (to be developed in Chapter 8).

"Intrinsic prior knowledge" is the knowledge that listeners have gained from what has gone before this utterance in the text being listened to. For example, if in an earlier part of the same text learners have ascertained both that an individual was found guilty of a particular charge and that they were listening to a report on a court case, then they would be able to make some well-based guesses as to what would follow; for example, it might be a statement of the punishment given by the court. Activities should be developed to train students to do this type of guessing. (This will be developed further in Chapter 8.) Note that in this kind of activity, students are drawing on prior knowledge *from within the text*. They then graft that onto what they know from their world knowledge about reporting on court cases ("extrinsic world knowledge") in order to put all this together. This also links with the identification of the genre or rhetorical form that they are listening to (also discussed in Chapter 8).

World knowledge is of vital importance not only in assisting listeners in narrowing down the possibilities and guessing, but also in knowing how to interpret the illocutionary force of a particular utterance. Richards (1983:221) makes the distinction between "propositional meaning" and "illocutionary force" as it pertains to listening. He gives the example of the utterance "Helen likes chocolates," pointing out that while the propositional meaning may be clear—attributing a certain quality to Helen—it does not tell us whether this is an explanation of her obesity, or a suggestion what to do with the chocolates. Only previous knowledge of some kind can make this clear to listeners.

7.5. Discourse Markers

Discourse markers can also lead to the essence of an utterance. As was described in Section 5.7, there are certain discourses markers that "flag" or signal what the discourse is that will follow. When trying to get at the essence of the meaning of an utterance, students should be trained to notice and process the discourse markers. For example, "on the other hand" at the start of an utterance tells listeners that the next point will be the converse of the one just mentioned. Hearing "in other words" is a signal that a paraphrase is coming, meaning that if the previous utterance was clear, then this is a time when listeners can relax for a moment. If, on the other hand, the previous utterance was *not* clear, then this is a "second chance," and it will probably be couched in simpler language. Students should also be trained to take advantage of discourse markers as "landmarks" in passages of spoken language that are often not very well organized. These markers become explicit signals or guides as to the organization.

It has been my experience that the best way to convince students to use discourse markers is by developing activities that do and do not have discourse markers, leading learners to a realization that their presence helps a great deal in comprehension. For example:

1. A polyglot is a person who knows many languages. On the other hand, a linguist is a person who studies the structure of language.

2. I believe that this is the best. It is imported.

3. I believe that this is the best. What is more, it is imported.

4. I believe that this is the best. However, it is imported.

In Example 1, processing "on the other hand" immediately tells listeners that what is to follow will not be the same as what preceded it, immediately making it clear that "polyglot" and "linguist" are not synonyms. In Example 2, there is some ambiguity or lack of clarity as to the total meaning of the discourse, due to the absence of a discourse marker. In Examples 3 and 4, this is made clear, yielding two very different meanings.

7.6. Concluding Comments

Traditionally, the types of strategies and activities that have been described in this chapter are sorely neglected when teaching listening comprehension. I believe that this derives from two sources: first, an insecurity on the part of many teachers as to how the stress/unstress system works, and the way information is structured into units and how this relates to the intonational units in English; second, an insecurity, also on the part of teachers, as to how these seemingly theoretical facts can and should be applied in the ESL classroom. As has been shown, in fact there is much that second-language learners can gain from using these strategies, and it is not as complex as it seems.

Hypothesis Formation, Predicting, and Inferencing

8.1. Introductory Comments and Definitions

In the previous chapters, I have described different strategies to determine such things as setting, topic, etc., using all the reliable linguistic, paralinguistic, and extralinguistic signals available to the listener. In this chapter, the goal is to use whatever information these strategies have yielded to bring all this together. The hope is that second-language listeners will draw on all of those "pieces of the puzzle," and then apply strategies of hypothesis formation, predicting, and inferencing, which will be described in this chapter. This should lead them to a viable (and, we hope, correct) understanding of what they have been listening to. Note that this is top-down processing.

Hypothesis formation and hypothesis modification is at the root of both predicting and inferencing. The idea is that listeners should form a hypothesis as early on in the listening as possible (or preferably even before beginning to listen by means of the prelistening), and then either confirm or modify it as greater knowledge becomes available. Gillian Brown (1990:167) makes the very insightful point that in real life, probably many times a day, listeners in their first language form incorrect hypotheses, but often they never find this out, as the opportunity for correction just does not arise. Unless they are corrected, they carry on, assuming that they were correct. Second-language listeners must be encouraged to do the same.

In this chapter, I will be using the term "guessing" as a superordinate or more general term to encompass the more specific concepts of "predicting" and "inferencing."

8.1.1. Predicting

When learners have a certain amount but not all of the information (either because only part of the whole passage has been heard so far or because only a part has been comprehended), they should try to guess the total meaning—

this is "predicting." For example, identifying that speakers are in an airport and identifying the words *fog, flight,* and *late* should make it possible to predict the shape of the whole passage. Or, if students hear, "Noa was so happy with the wonderful gift from her parents. She had wanted one all her life. She ran up to her father and . . ." they should be able to predict with some certainty the completion of the discourse—they might not predict the exact words, but they could probably predict what Noa did next. The whole *purpose* of a strategy-based approach to listening comprehension is to get learners to use strategies that will increase the probability of their being able to tell what it is they are listening to on the basis of as intelligent a prediction and/or inference as possible.

8.1.2. Inferencing

"Inferencing," on the other hand, is more subtle, and, in some senses, a "higher level" of processing than predicting. In the case of inferencing, unlike when predicting, everything is comprehensible, but there is meaning to the discourse that exceeds the understanding of each of the utterances or parts of it. Adding these together, only by inferencing will the *whole* be comprehended. Inferencing is linked, then, to Canale and Swain's (1980) notion of "competence for discourse." For example, a news report might contain the following information:

> The number of cancer-related deaths has increased by 35% over the past five years.
>
> The price of cigarettes is being doubled as of January.

Competent listeners would assume that these are not simply two unrelated news items, but that there is a very clear relationship between them. This is a very sound assumption that is seldom wrong—it is uncommon for two propositions to be randomly placed next to each other. However, the relationship that exists is very often not made explicit in the language, and that is what can throw second-language learners. They may be able to comprehend the first proposition, and the second, but miss the causal relationship between them.

In a second example, the passage might be the following:

MAN: That damned cat, Cinderella, has been locked out again.

WOMAN: I'm already in bed.

Of course we can never be sure what the outcome of this exchange will be, but competent listeners would understand the man's utterance to be an appeal to the woman to let the cat in, and the woman's response to be a refusal. We can infer from the exchange that the man will be the one to let the cat in. This ability to make inferences draws very heavily on our world and cultural knowledge—if, for example, we were functioning in a culture in which women were expected to do everything domestic and men absolutely nothing, we would make a very different inference as to what would come next.

8.2. Creating the Atmosphere for Guessing

Guessing meaning or intent requires taking risks. It is a tantalizing fact that second-language learners are hesitant to predict and make inferences although this is something they do all the time when listening in their first language. Second-language listeners, as I have stated several times, tend to be very cautious when listening, and want to understand every single word. They are not willing to take the risks that predicting and inferencing require. The role of the second-language teacher in this regard is to get students to take that leap and to predict and inference. This can be achieved by the teacher taking a number of steps.

8.2.1. Convincing the Students that "It is Good to Guess"

Students need to be convinced of this. "It is good to guess" is the motto of my ESL listening classes, and I play up this point from the very first class. Many students come into ESL classes from fairly conservative education systems in which they are told repeatedly not to guess. While it is clear that such an injunction makes perfect sense in certain circumstances, particularly as an alternative to preparing homework, guessing clearly has its place in the listening class, and reeducation about guessing is often necessary. As far back as 1975, Rubin, in her early work, was suggesting that the good language learner is a good guesser. However, students will only be willing to take the risk and to guess if the atmosphere is supportive enough, and if they see the payoff.

8.2.2. Convincing the Students that Nothing Terrible Happens when They are Wrong

Through discussion and strategy training, students need to be persuaded to take the leap that predicting and inferencing require, with the understanding that this is *not blind guessing* of the type that they were forbidden to do at school. This is more a case of presuming the whole, on the basis of a part, or making assumptions by linking what they have heard with what they know about that topic. They have to be convinced that the risk they are being asked to take is minimal, both because more often than not they will be correct, and because of the supportive atmosphere that the teacher has created in the listening class.

As was stated when discussing the nature of the listening process inChapter 1, teachers and students of listening have to adjust their thinking about listening comprehension, and to stop thinking in terms of *absolutely correct* comprehension, but rather in terms of listening leading to an *interpretation* of meaning. Moreover, they have to become accustomed to the fact that guessing, i.e., making a hypothesis, is not a final unchangeable decision. It is *expected* of students that they will modify their hypotheses (many times if necessary) as more   becomes clear, and this is a natural way to process listening.

Finally, the myth perpetuated by some teachers that if learners are encouraged to guess, then they will stop listening to the words, also has to be dispelled. Perhaps the most powerful way of all to convince students and resistant teachers alike that it is good to guess when listening is to provide activities that prove the effectiveness of these "guessing strategies."

8.2.3. Creating a Supportive Atmosphere in the Classroom for Guessing

A supportive atmosphere is absolutely essential in the listening class. In a second-language setting, there are ample opportunities to try things out in an unsupportive atmosphere. From the outset, it is vital that students and teacher contract deliberately and explicitly to be supportive of all class members, and that every effort be made to prevent anyone ever being laughed at for their efforts. Much of this depends on the example set by the teacher and by the way he or she handles any inappropriate behavior from a student. The class should know that they will always be commended for trying and for guessing, even if it turns out that they are wrong. This has to be worked at by the teacher and students from the very first lesson.

In my classes, I discuss this very frankly with the class on the first day while raising their consciousness as to what we do when we listen, and informing them of what we will be doing.

8.3. Background Knowledge for Predicting and Inferencing

Background or world knowledge, as has been discussed, is extremely important in being able to make predictions and inferences. In Section 7.4, I made the distinction between what I call "extrinsic world knowledge" and "intrinsic world knowledge." Intrinsic world knowledge is knowledge listeners have from what has already been heard, i.e., the knowledge comes from within the text itself. Extrinsic world knowledge is knowledge learners have of the topic in question before ever beginning to listen to this text. In the literature, the terms "background knowledge" or "world knowledge" are usually equivalent to my "extrinsic world knowledge." For example, if students know that a passage is going to be about "tax shelters," and some of them know what tax shelters are, they will immediately be able to make predictions about what is going to be heard. Other students, who do not know what "tax shelters" are, will not be able to make such predictions, and the listening task will be much more difficult for them. As Gillian Brown (1990:155) points out, "The problem for foreign learners is that so much 'familiar knowledge' has to be established from scratch. They have to find out what, of their already existing familiar knowledge, can safely be imported."

As I have stated, prelistening activities are very important to activate existing schemata. An additional very important value of prelistening activities is that they help to "level the playing field" somewhat—to provide some common core of world knowledge for all students before the listening itself. Of course, this does not completely level out the differences, but it does help. Subsequently, both kinds of world knowledge should work in conjunction with the signals available from the passage, yielding comprehension.

Making correct inferences is equally or even more dependent on world knowledge as is making predictions—the prior knowledge enables listeners to listen "between the lines," beyond the actual words that are heard.

8.4. Predicting

As was mentioned above, predicting is very important in listening comprehension. What competent listeners normally do is not to predict the exact words that the speaker is going to say (nor is this important), but rather to predict the idea that is going to be presented. This is something that people do all the time in their own language, evidenced by the fact that it is not uncommon for people to react to an utterance before it is complete, to end their interlocutor's sentence for them, or to end it along with them.

Second-language speakers must be persuaded to make predictions in the second language like they do so naturally in the first. This can be achieved by making the act of predicting a *conscious* one.

Predicting is generally based on all or some of the following: on the basis of the world knowledge that we bring to that particular topic; on the basis of what has preceded the section being listened to; and on the basis of the signals that we have been able to identify (Mendelsohn 1984). When we speak of drawing on world knowledge, we are referring to the content schema that has to be activated. O'Malley et al. (1989:421) describe this activation of propositions and schemata as follows: "Connections between the new text meaning and existing knowledge occur through *spreading activation* in which knowledge in long-term memory is activated to the degree that it is related to the new meanings in short-term memory." Richards (1983) provides an extended example of the prior knowledge that can be activated when hearing an utterance—what he calls "script knowledge"— see below.

There is also a very important additional aspect of world knowledge that should be drawn on when predicting, and that is knowledge of the *genre*, of the accepted formula or rhetorical pattern of a particular piece of discourse—also known as a "textual schema" or "rhetorical schema" (see Section 1.3). For example, a piece of discourse may be in the form of a claim supported by data or facts. The shape of such a discourse would be quite different from a passage giving instructions as to how to do something, or a narration of events. Gillian Brown and George Yule (1983:62) suggest thinking of genre in terms of three "levels": the "larger" genre, e.g., a church service; a small-scale generic event, e.g., a prayer; and the microevent, e.g., a vocative expression.

Second-language learners have a tendency to ignore the issue of genres with their conventional organizational patterns, thereby missing a very helpful way of getting at, for example, the main point in relation to secondary points, and of being able to predict what is to come. If, for example, learners grasp that they are listening to someone arguing a point (the "thesis" or main idea), and that this is being substantiated by two sets of data, then exactly how each utterance fits into the total passage immediately becomes much clearer. In addition, the different genres, and the different parts of the genres have "cue words" such as *in contrast, once upon a time,* or *but the most compelling reason is* . . .which are very valuable signals to the listener.

Making use of genre identification when predicting is a good example of top-down processing in listening. Of course, its value depends on how much cuing is present, and how well organized the spoken discourse is.

Important linguistic signals for predicting are also available through intonation and stress. Competent listeners will know the implication of a fall-rise tone on "nice" in an utterance like, "True, that table's very nice." They will be able to predict explicitly or implicitly that what will follow will be a "but" clause in contradiction of the statement that it is very nice; for example, " . . . but the price is too high." Similarly, identification of primary sentence stress and the communicative importance of why it occurs where it does leads competent listeners to important predictions (see Chapter 7).

Another linguistic signal which is useful for predicting is recognizing what other lexical items a particular lexical item most commonly collocates with. For example, the verb "to cash" usually collocates with a limited set of items like "check" or "money order." Similarly, "to run for" usually collocates with something like "political office" (although, of course, it could also be "to run for a bus or a train").

8.5. Inferencing

In Section 1.4, I described listening as an interpretive process. Inferencing is an important and necessary part of that interpretive process that leads to comprehension. In effect, what we are doing is making certain assumptions based on the information we have.

Gillian Brown (1990:168) suggests the following processes through which an utterance is interpreted. They show the place and importance of inferencing very clearly:

> *Before* the utterance, drawing on world knowledge, the listener predicts; *during* the utterance, the listener *builds* on this prediction using the available signals; *after* the utterance, the listener works out what was meant, i.e. he/she *infers* the meaning.

This also relates to the notion of *scripts* (a subset of schemata) and the way we store certain things in long-term memory:

> Much of our knowledge of the world is organized around scripts, that is, memory for typical episodes that occur in specific situations. . . . The information needed to understand many utterances is therefore not explicitly present in the utterance but is provided by the listeners from their repertoire of scripts. This means that many of the connections between events need not be specified when we talk about them,

since they are already known and can be inferred. But if we lack a relevant script, comprehension may be difficult. (Richards 1983:223)

Richards exemplifies this notion with the following piece of discourse: "I went to the dentist this morning. He gave me an injection and I didn't feel a thing."

He then explains what knowledge is needed to fully comprehend this:

1. We normally go to see a dentist when we need a check-up or when we have something wrong with our teeth.

2. Dentists typically check, drill, repair or remove teeth.

3. This process is painful.

4. An injection can be given to relieve pain.

(p. 222)

Note that it is our "script knowledge" that enables us to get the full meaning of the discourse.

Trying to comprehend a passage that we do not have a relevant script or schema for is difficult even for a native speaker, and many scripts and schemata are culture-specific, compounding the difficulty for ESL students.

Perhaps the most important thing that we need to get across to second-language listeners is that it is the norm that not everything is said explicitly so that even if they hear and understand every word, this will not guarantee total comprehension. Our task is to bring this fact to a conscious level, thereby reducing the anxiety level of learners trying to understand every word and every detail. Everyone makes inferences and guesses in their first language—the key is to train students to take that leap in the second language.

8.6. Strategies and Activities for Predicting and Inferencing

As was described above, when predicting and inferencing, learners are pulling together everything covered in the preceding chapters. In this section I will suggest a number of activities for guessing (some involving predicting, some inferencing, and some a combination of the two), the goal being to help students gain confidence to apply these strategies in their learning. It is encouraging to note that prelistening and subsequent predicting and inferencing are beginning to be more commonplace in ESL listening texts.[15]

A procedure that I have found effective in encouraging students to predict and inference, drawing on their prior knowledge, is to do some prelistening in the form of a group discussion. The group's input is particularly helpful to those students who may lack the relevant schemata. After the discussion and the predicting (including, as always, discussion on how they arrived at their predictions), students begin to listen to a passage; however, halfway through

---

[15] Kellerman's (1922a) observation from examining five British textbooks published in the last five years.

the passage, the tape is stopped and the students hold a discussion as to what they think will be contained in the rest of the passage, similar to the confidence-building activity below.

8.6.1. A Confidence-Building Activity

It is very important to provide activities that will help to boost students' confidence. Ellis and Sinclair (1989a) offer a very sensible "confidence-building" activity for learners trying to understand the news. They suggest that learners first listen to the news in their own language, look at a newspaper in their own language, list the topics they think will probably be in the news, and finally choose two topics that they are most interested in and make notes as to what they think will be said about these points. Then, while listening, they check their predictions. This kind of activity is very helpful, and reduces the danger of students simply giving up. This kind of very supportive and encouraging activity is advisable at the beginning of a strategy-based course.

8.6.2. A Hypothesis-Formation/Hypothesis-Modification Activity

Very early on in a listening course, I carry out a training activity aimed at teaching students how important it is to formulate a hypothesis as quickly as possible, and how completely natural and common it is that their hypotheses might require modification when more information is clear. The following is an example that I have used in my classes.

I have an authentic audio recording of an operation being performed in an operating theater, and I divide it into four sections:

1. There is a tapping noise, the tapping being at regular intervals.

2. The rhythm of the tapping changes and becomes less regular.

3. The words, "Yes, I think I'll take a little piece off here" are heard, said in quite a bored, off-hand way.

4. There is much "medical talk," including words like, *bone wax*, *granuloma*, and *put in a drip*, making it clear that this is an operation.

I make it clear to the students that they are going to hear the tape in four parts, and that after each part they must say what it is that they are listening to, and more importantly, how they arrived at their hypotheses.

I play Segment 1 to the students. They are asked what they think they are listening to, and we discuss how they arrived at their hypotheses. Many students zero in on the regularity of the tapping and suggest that it is a metronome while others simply think it is some form of hammering, or chiseling, or the sound of someone walking.

On playing Segment 2, the "metronomists" modify their hypotheses due to the irregularity of the tapping. They tend to modify their hypotheses to one of the others already stated. Most of the "non-metronomist" students choose not to modify their hypotheses at this point.

On playing Segment 3, many students think that they are listening to an artist at work on a piece of sculpture. They explain that the words that they hear lead them to this hypothesis. The words clearly call for a modification in hypothesis by those who thought it was the sound of walking, and the words they hear and the tone of the words lead them to the "artist-at-work" hypothesis. It is very interesting to note that although I have tried this passage with hundreds of native and non-native speakers, I have *never* had anyone hypothesize at this stage that this is the sound of a surgeon at work. The reason for this would seem to be that those words with that tone do *not* fit with the scripts that most of us have for what transpires in an operating theater—clearly very different from the television script for an operation! Most people have never watched a surgeon at work, and what scripts they have are often fictional media representations of reality.

The speed with which listeners ultimately clue into what they really are listening to is determined by their ability to recognize the medical terms used in Segment 4.

This activity is very good training in hypothesis-formation/hypothesis modification because it is virtually certain that as the discourse progresses, it will be necessary to modify the hypothesis. My experience has been that this kind of discourse, with a surprise element or twist is very good for raising students' awareness of what they should be doing and why.

Rubin (1988) has a similar activity, only she begins by having students predict what a video is about based only on the title. It has been my experience that this kind of conscious discussion and prediction on the basis of the title is very useful, as the title of a passage is very revelatory, and second-language learners tend to ignore titles.

8.6.3. An Utterance Completion Activity

A training activity that I have found valuable is what I call "utterance completion." It is very effective in encouraging students to guess and can be used at a relatively low level of proficiency. Students hear half utterances like the following and are asked to complete them:

1. My sister did very well on her report card. However, I . . .

2. One of the demonstrators just fired his gun at the police. One of the police officers has . . .

3. My friend went, but I . . .

4. He said he would do it. However, . . .

5. He said he would do it although . . .

6. He said he would do it and . . .

Utterances 1–3 have a rather limited number of possible completions. Utterances 4–6 are more complex, because although the *however, although* and the *and* tell competent listeners what the relationship between the propositions will be, the details are much more open-ended. For example, in Utterance 4, it is clear that he did not do it, but the nature of what will follow is not. It could be as different as, "He said he would do it. However, he was lying," as opposed to, "He said he would do it. However, the hurricane made it impossible."

Extensive work on predicting and how we make well-based predictions can be done with sets of utterances like 4–6.

The same thing can be done with more sophisticated utterances like the following:

7. At the lecture, one or two people asked questions, but . . .

8. A woman was hit by a bicycle outside the supermarket and all her . . .

9. In spite of the warning, . . .

Examples with increasing options should also be used so as to show students how often they can still be correct, and how getting it wrong is not so terrible. These can be opened up until very open examples are given like Utterance 9. Clearly, there is not enough information here to be able to predict what the following proposition will be. It could be, " . . . the widow went to the apartment alone." On the other hand, it could be something as different as, ". . . I consented." Because the possibilities are so large, I see a value in training students to predict, but to be ready to make modifications.[16]

8.6.4. A "What Will Happen Next?" Activity

A more sophisticated version of the activity described in Section 8.6.3, which combines predicting and inferencing, is one that I call "What will happen next?" Students hear exchanges like the following, and are asked to say what will happen next or what will be said next, and how they arrived at their decision:

A: I really need a new outfit for the party.

B: But you bought a new outfit just last month.

A: Yes, but that was for casual use. What I need now is something more formal. This is a formal dinner with all my colleagues.

B: Well I think it's ridiculous.

WHAT WILL HAPPEN NEXT?

---

[16] Ur (1984) has similar activities in which students fill in the gaps in a dialogue.

8.6.5. A "What Did She Say?" Activity

This is very good for training students to guess. Basically, what happens is that students work in pairs, and listen to utterances with parts made inaudible by turning the sound down or by editing in white noise (static). One student asks the other, "What did she say?" and the other student tells him or her, guessing the missing parts. For example, they might hear passages like the following, in which ##### represents inaudible segments of varying lengths:

1. Jason has been very ill. His lungs are #####, making it very hard for him to #####.

2. My aunt has just returned from a long holiday. She looks very ##### and #####. She's going back to work this week. I fear that by next week she'll feel ##### and look ##### again.

Examples like Utterance 2 can be quite difficult. I have, on occasion, provided students with a list of possible options. However, what I have found to be much more successful and valuable is to discuss with students what types of words or expressions would fit into the different slots, and why. Usually they are clear that the first two will probably be positive adjectives such as "well" and "rested," based on our world knowledge of the positive value of holidays to health. The last two will probably not be positive, based largely on the word "fear." We then discuss how they arrived at that conclusion, bringing to a conscious level the importance of the signal contained in the word "fear." Ultimately, students realize that they are in fact better able to predict the missing bits than they thought, and that although they might not have got the exact words in any of the slots, they likely got the main idea, and that is what is most important.

A variation on this activity is one I call "I could barely hear anything." Here, too, not everything is clear, and in fact almost everything is made inaudible. A few key lexical items, and some background noise are all that is clear. For example, students would hear the following:

1. [Sound of telephones and office noise] ############## type ############## report ############## San Francisco, please.

2. [Crowd noise at a sporting event] ############## Montreal ############## badly.

3. [Organ music playing "Mendelssohn's Wedding March"] ############## caught a thief ############## store ##############.

4. [Crowd noise at a sporting event] ############## movie ############## boring ##############.

Here, students should be encouraged to make use of all the signals available, but in utterances 3 and 4, the extralinguistic signals have been *deliberately* chosen as they do not lead to a correct hypothesis. This is intended to train students to be on their guard, since not all signals lead to correct predictions. Variations on this type of activity are possible focusing, for example, on the words containing stressed syllables.

8.6.6. An "Eavesdropping" Activity

Porter and Roberts (1981:46) describe an "eavesdropping" activity aimed at encouraging guessing. Listeners eavesdrop on a series of short conversations at a party. They are asked to guess what the people are talking about, and to write down whether they would like to join any of the conversations. The important difference between this activity and those listed above is that here students listen from the middle of a text—something that in real life native speakers often have to do.

8.6.7. A "Listening Between the Lines" Activity

Lougheed (1985) has developed some very clever inferencing activities (advanced level) in which a very short and rapid exchange is heard, but the dialogue is deliberately structured to be ambiguous, and only judicious inferencing makes it possible to get at the actual meaning. Not only does this textbook provide a large number of very cleverly thought out exchanges, but it also trains students how to make inferences through a series of questions about the passage. These questions, in effect, constitute a checklist, or a guide to inferencing. Students find this very difficult at first, but with practice, it becomes much easier and, what is more, they then find it a lot of fun. Lougheed's are true training activities focused directly on inferencing.

8.7. Concluding Comments

Guessing in the form of hypothesis formation, predicting, and inferencing is absolutely essential if our students are to become competent listeners. Spoken language is comprehensible to competent listeners precisely because they do not try to listen and process word-by-word. What is more, not everything that is being conveyed in an utterance or a passage is said explicitly, and, if it were, then passages would have to be much longer in order to convey the same propositions. This means that inferencing is vital for competent listeners. It is for this reason that developing strategies that lead into a practice of predicting and inferencing is at the root of the strategy-based approach that I am advocating for teaching listening comprehension.

Listening to Different Things in Different Ways

9.1. Introductory Comments

All too often, the fact that we listen to different things in different ways is overlooked in listening courses for second-language speakers and the courses tend to be monolithic, implying that there is one way to listen to everything. The variety that does exist in these courses is usually variety in the passages to be listened to, not variety in the tasks, nor in the *types* of passages. It has long been recognized in the other receptive skill, reading comprehension, that we need to read different things in different ways, but this has only recently begun to be acknowledged and acted upon in listening courses. We have to train our students to listen to different things in different ways, and this will affect both the nature and length of the passages that we use, and the tasks that are based on them.[17]

A by-product of recognizing the need to listen to different things in different ways is that it rules out the "formulaic" fixed-format lesson of listening courses, and this, in turn, ensures variation and reduces tedium.

One of the most serious weaknesses that I see in traditional listening comprehension courses is that the tasks are inappropriate for the kind of listening that was being done, and this often had the negative effect of requiring students to listen in a way that was not suitable for the passage in question—in fact, teaching them bad listening comprehension habits. For example, students would be required to listen to a lengthy passage (no indication of the type of task/s that were to follow, no training or even suggestion that they take notes) and then asked to answer questions on minutiae. Not only does this place an impossible burden on memory, but it bears little or no relation to what people listen to and how they listen in the real world.

---

[17] See Prabhu's (1987) three types of tasks: information-gap, opinion-gap, and reasoning-gap.

When planning a listening comprehension course, it must be borne in mind that the listening that we do takes place in two different forms:

i. *Two-way communication*—in dialogues or on the telephone, usually taking the form of what Gillian Brown and George Yule (1983) call "language for interactional purposes," for example, in small talk when the focus is not on the information or content.[18] Because this communication is two-way, there can be a negotiation and elicitation of meaning, and there is a whole subset of sociolinguistic and discourse rules for such negotiation and elicitation. Much of what learners have to master in order to elicit help and negotiate meaning in a participatory dialogue belongs in a book on speaking rather than on listening, and will only be addressed very briefly in this book (see Section 9.9). However, even in lecture settings, students should be allowed and encouraged to ask questions.

ii. *One-way communication*—for example, in a lecture or while watching television—"language for transactional purposes" (Gillian Brown and George Yule 1983). Richards (1990:62–65) provides a useful list of exercises that involve listening for interactional purposes and exercises that involve listening for transactional purposes.

The person developing a listening course must determine what kinds of listening their learners need. This will determine the kinds of listening that should be included in the course or textbook.

In addition to encouraging our students to listen to different things in different ways, we have to recognize that this entails *understanding* different things differently as well. For example, understanding directions as to how to get to some place is very different from what it means to understand a piece on the radio, where all that is called for is that listeners gets the gist of what is being said. This must be borne in mind as we design listening comprehension courses, and, in fact, it should dictate the nature of the tasks and the teacher's expectations.

An additional variable in the types of listening that we train our students in, is the question of the accents or dialects of English that learners are exposed to. Practicality normally dictates that, initially at least, the main exposure will be to the accent of the teacher and/or the dominant dialect of English for that region (in a second-language setting) or for that educational system (in a foreign language setting). There is, of course, the problem, particularly in most English as a *foreign* language situations, that many of the teachers are non-native speakers themselves. In these situations, it is advisable that the teacher provide a lot of opportunities to students to listen to recorded speech of native speakers of English. However, even when the teacher is a native speaker, the question of exposure to other accents must be addressed. I believe that at the

---

[18] Rost (1990) calls this "collaborative discourse"; Joiner (1991) uses the term, "two-way interactive listening."

lower levels, students should mainly be exposed to one dialect, but that exposure to different accents should be deliberately built into more advanced listening courses. In today's "global village," we owe this to our students as much as we owe exposing them to real spoken language.

In this chapter, I will spell out the main types of listening that we traditionally do, and will suggest principles of material selection and grading, and activities to train students in these different types of listening. However, from the outset, it is important to emphasize that the various types of listening that we do are not necessarily done separately from each other, although it might appear that way from their presentation here—the separation into discrete categories is for the purposes of emphasis and pedagogic clarity.

The following is a list of the main types of listening that we do, all or part of which will likely be included in second-language listening comprehension courses. The list is not presented in order of importance, nor is it intended to be definitive, because that is something that can only be determined according to the needs of the particular listeners.

- Listening for academic content, plus note-taking (e.g., lectures)

- Listening for one crucial detail (e.g., flight arrival time)

- Listening for *all* the details (e.g., getting directions)

- Listening for relaxation and pleasure (e.g., movies)

- Listening for the gist (e.g., unplanned radio listening)

- Listening for mood and atmosphere (e.g., to decide what is going on between speakers)

- Listening on the telephone (to different types of conversations)

- Listening for interactional purposes

9.2. Academic Listening

Academic listening involves *listening in order to learn*, while most of what is done in traditional listening comprehension courses is *listening in order to understand*, even in courses whose goal is to train students in English for academic purposes.

Comprehending lectures is a very important part of academics—Johnstone (1963, cited in Verner and Dickinson 1967) found that 10.5% of all participation in organized educational activities of American adults was in lectures. In the past twenty years or so, numerous academic listening courses for second-language learners have begun to appear on the market, and this is a very important step forward. However, there are often a number of problems with such courses. The following are the main ones:

- *The level of the content*. For many students it is either too technical or too puerile. It is extremely difficult to plan a "prepackaged" listening course that will suit the knowledge level, let alone the linguistic level, of all students.

- *The decontextualized nature of the lectures.* ESL academic listening courses tend to take the form of listening to a selection of lectures and performing certain tasks based on them. However, the academic reality is that outside of the "guest lecture," students are usually required to listen to a *series* of lectures on a topic, which together build up a complete picture. Lectures given in a series or as part of an academic course vary substantially from what we usually find in most ESL academic listening courses. These tend more to approximate the guest lecture in scope, organization and structure.

- *Lectures tend to be written discourse which is being read.* Although we have come a long way in teaching listening and in our understanding of the unique nature of spoken English, this is often not carried over to the academic lectures in ESL courses. The reasons for this are logistical rather than pedagogic, but this does not alter the fact that this makes them unnatural and cognitively more difficult than real spoken lectures. They tend to share much with the conference paper that is read aloud.

- *Seldom is there training in how to use the notes that have been taken.* This is usually the case even when the course includes training in note-taking. This point will be developed below.

- *The listening task in the ESL program tends to be "listening only."* In reality, academic listening invariably requires that listening be integrated with other skills. The need for integration with the other skills becomes apparent when we consider what it is students listen to lectures for and what they do with their notes (see Benson 1989:423).

Academic listening is not merely one of the eight main types of listening that I have identified. It is somewhat special because of the uniqueness of the situation in which it usually takes place, and also because one of the goals is actually *listening to learn* and not just listening to comprehend. In his research, Benson (1989) found that the gap between the lower level "listening to comprehend" of the intensive English Program and the "listening to learn" of the real academic course was enormous. Quite apart from the fact that in the academic course there is the issue of grades, what the learner has to do in such a course is different and more extensive: "His [the learner's] need was to get hold not merely of some facts but also of the attitudes that underlay their selection and presentation. He was, in fact, listening to learn . . . listening as practiced in the university is both quantitatively and qualitatively different from listening within the ESL classroom" (p. 441, 422). What is more, most ESL academic listening passages fail to recognize that lectures vary greatly both in the degree of formality (Dudley-Evans and Johns 1981) and in speaker style (George Brown and Bakhtar 1983, cited in Rost 1990:161; Beebe 1985).

Academic listening requires that learners listen, take notes, participate in class discussion, and link what they have heard with their prior knowledge of the topic and often also with further knowledge, for example through their reading. Clearly, what we should be striving for in the academic listening course is to train students to do precisely that (see Ruetten 1986). This requires that comprehensive units of material with serious and varied content (in outlook, format, etc.) be prepared, and that students also be trained how to tackle the different parts of this complex task of learning by listening. Failure to train students how to do this turns this academic listening into what I have characterized as a testing and retesting situation.

How to prepare students to handle lectures is a question not easily answered. Snow and Perkins (1979) advocate beginning with "academic interviews," so that the interviewer can "guide the expert" (p. 53). This provides some control during the training period.

One of the strategies that students can use to help them to understand lectures is making maximum use of the discourse markers. Yuan (1982:48, cited in Chaudron and Richards 1986) found that second-language students do not pay attention to discourse markers, and are much more concerned with "decoding the speech sentence by sentence." Chaudron and Richards' (1986) study shows that the "macro structure" discourse markers are very helpful for successful recall of a lecture. These are the "higher-order discourse markers signalling major transitions and emphasis in the lecture" (p. 123), for example, "What I'm going to talk about today . . .; Let's go back to the beginning . . .;" and "This brought about new problems . . ." (p. 117). Identification of such markers triggers expectations and predictions.

Yuan's and Chaudron and Richards' studies both call for the training of students in recognizing and making use of macro discourse markers.[19]

9.2.1. Note-taking

Note-taking is a very important part of academic listening and requires careful attention in any English for Academic Purposes (EAP) ESL course. However, taking notes shifts the focus from the text to the taking of the notes (Rost 1990). Therefore, skillful note-takers need to use shorthand and/or other techniques to get down the main points without losing focus on the text. While it is agreed that there are many different ways of taking notes—in diagram form, in full words, in various types of shorthand, in "T-formation" notes (Hamp-Lyons 1983), using flow charts, and in semantic maps and tree diagrams (Oxford 1990)—one thing is clear: students attending academic courses that include lectures need to be able to take notes so that they have a record to refer back to.

---

[19] For an example of a text that trains students to identify such markers, see Young and Fitzgerald (1982).

Spearrit (1962), citing McClendon's (1957) findings, points out that results are not affected by the actual type of note-taking done, and so students should be encouraged to use whatever system suits them, and ESL courses should not push for one specific format. Lecturers seldom provide their students with a lecture outline, which, by definition, would identify the main points, and students are left to make of the lecture what they can and to note what *they* judge to be important. Therefore, students in an ESL academic listening course need to be trained to take notes and to be given a lot of practice in this difficult skill. One very helpful finding from the empirical literature is that good, experienced listeners will take notes first and foremost in accordance with what they think they will be expected to be able to do with this information (Dunkel 1985; Chaudron, Cook, and Loschky 1988). This reinforces the importance of informing students in advance as to what they should be listening for, and this, in turn, provides a valuable guide as to how to train students in note-taking.

Benson (1989) did an in depth study of the listening comprehension of a Saudi Arabian graduate student, Hamad, and his findings are very revelatory. Hamad tended to note only the main or general statements, and to ignore subsidiary points and examples, so that his notes tended to be incomplete, when compared with the notes of a top native speaker. He also ignored metaphors and items where language was likely a problem even though these might have been major points. As well, Benson found that Hamad tended to take very few notes based on interactions during the lectures. I would suspect that the same holds true for most native speakers—it is my experience that the rest of the class tends to "switch off" while a question is being asked and answered. This can result in important points being overlooked. Finally, Hamad's notes expressed "a Saudi Arabian viewpoint," evidenced in the way in which the lecture content was related to prior knowledge. Benson also notes, when comparing this real academic note-taking with ESL listening course note-taking, that in the real situation, the fact that the teacher was also the person who set the examinations and assigned the grades, significantly influenced Hamad's note-taking.

As I stated above, taking notes, however comprehensive they may be, is not an end in itself, although it would seem so from some ESL listening courses. The real "litmus test" is whether learners are able to do with the notes the academic tasks that they are assigned, not whether they can take notes per se. Students need to be able to take notes in as much detail and in whatever form best suits them, so that they can use them later as an aid to memory. It is really impossible to prescribe, for example how much is enough, or how much is too much.

I have, on a number of occasions, attempted to take this very important point into consideration in my ESL listening courses, deliberately creating a time gap and then giving an academic task drawing on the notes. While this brings us closer to academic reality, the fact that the task was ungraded and part of a noncredit general proficiency ESL course made it rather artificial.

Benson's minicourses described below follow the same principles but address some of the weaknesses I encountered.

Early on in an academic listening course, the teacher should clarify the task that is to come and give students a passage to listen to and take notes on, and then hold a consciousness-raising discussion on what they did and did not note down and why. When discussing activities for note-taking, it must be assumed that all of the appropriate strategies that have already been proposed for general listening will be applied. For example, as discussed above, the identification of discourse markers is *extremely* helpful.

As training for more unguided note-taking, students can be asked to fill in partial outlines, in which actual words from the text cue them. An alternative type of preparatory activity is chart completion, but here there is the danger that this might degenerate into an exercise in "precision listening" for minute detail, for example, for diagram labeling purposes, and this may not be the type of task that would normally go with this type of text at all.

A slightly more difficult type of note-taking activity (and there are numerous variations that can be applied) is having students build up an outline to the lecture. This can be done by providing students with a skeleton, showing that there are, say, three main points, and that the first has four supporting points, the second has two, and the third has two. Students are then asked to fill in the skeleton. The same task of building up an outline *without* providing the skeleton is considerably more difficult although a skeleton can really confuse a student once they have made a mistake.

Getting down notes can be achieved in stages, beginning, for example, by training students to identify the thesis of an expository lecture. They can then be asked to listen to a lecture and afterwards be asked to imagine that, while waiting for a bus, they were chatting to a student who had missed the lecture. The discussion ran as follows:

Student who was present: "Today's was a really interesting lecture."

Student who was absent: "Really, what did she talk about?"

Student who was present: (sees the bus approaching) [Student has only twenty to thirty seconds to tell what it was about].

An activity of this kind forces students to zero in on the crux of the lecture.

9.2.2. "Content-Based" and "Simulated Content-Based" Courses

Recognition of the distinction between listening for comprehension in a regular ESL course, and listening to learn, raises the question as to how best to tackle academic listening. One of the options is content-based or "adjunct" courses for second-language learners, in which they are in fact enrolled in an academic course, with material they are required to learn, but with suitable language support. The underlying philosophy is that they will improve their language skills concurrently with learning the content. This approach is being used with a high level of success at a number of universities, for example, UCLA in the United States, and Ottawa and York universities in Canada. However, such an approach assumes a high-intermediate if not advanced level of proficiency, and leaves the question as to what to do to get students to this level. What I would propose is what has come to be called a "simulated content-based course." This is a course which is at a lower level than a real content-based course, and whose goal is to prepare students for their content courses. Such courses are offered very successfully at York University in Toronto.

At the root of a "simulated content-based course" is the fact that although this is first and foremost a language course, there is a body of material in some appropriate discipline that is going to be studied, and that this will provide training in academic listening. It is a "rehearsal" for content-based courses. The goal *must be* listening to learn, and the target *must be* handling the body of information. Benson (1989) calls these "minicourses" or "topic-centered modules," and points out that they lead to authentic note-taking: "The minicourse must be sufficiently long and detailed to recreate an authentic environment. A period of about seven weeks or around twenty contact hours, is suggested" (p. 441).

As will be discussed in Chapter 10, discussing academic listening immediately raises the issue of integrating listening with other language skills.

9.3. Listening for One Crucial Detail

This is one of what I call the "precision listening" skills. It is a very specific skill, parallel to the skill of reading for one particular detail. The more one thinks over the listening done by native speakers, the more one realizes the importance of such a skill. What is more, this kind of listening is often required by second-language speakers before their proficiency level is very high. Examples of this are listening to a recorded message on the telephone, or a loudspeaker announcement for particular flight details or where a delay has occurred on the subway line, or any other specific detail such as the temperature in one particular place. The common denominator is that the detail needed has to be pulled out of a larger set of details, *and is very important to that listener at that moment*. Another situation is related to listening for all the details (Section 9.4)— there are often cases in which it is necessary to listen for all the details, and listeners think they have got them all, but it then becomes evident that something has been missed. At this point, this, too becomes a case of listening for the one specific missing detail. Similarly, a person may be listening to a commercial for, say, a car, and may only want to know whether air conditioning is included in the price.

It would be an incomplete representation of this kind of listening to imply that it always involves extracting one detail from a list. There are often situations in which listeners are only concerned about one specific detail within the flow of speech that they are hearing, and they focus their listening on that alone. For example, a parent may be listening to a child recounting events that took place at school, and embedded in the account is the grade that the child got on a particular project. This may, in fact, be the only detail that the parent, supposedly listening to the whole account, is really listening for.

It might appear relatively simple to listen for one specific detail because listeners only need to pick out one point from the entire passage. However, what makes this quite difficult is that there may not be very clear signals of an acoustic or "discourse" type to guide listeners to the correct point. This is particularly problematic in cases like the child recounting what happened at school.

The strategy that I have trained my students to use is that of trying to determine, before listening, what the signals might be that would mark the item being listened for. The main strategy is one of "matching"—listening out for a word or proper noun that matches what they are listening for. Conversely, this requires that they activate what I call "rejecting strategies"—ways of knowing that the part they are listening to is *not* what they are after and can therefore be rejected. There is always the danger at these moments of letting attention wane and losing the point we were after! As with so many things in second-language listening, all we are doing is bringing to a conscious level what we do unconsciously in our first language.

If, for example, it is a list of flight arrival times that is being listened to, then the flight number is the obvious signal; if it is the weather, then it is the name of the area the listener is interested in. The "rejecting strategy" attached to this would be to listen for the system or order in which the flights are being listed. If, for example, they are being listed over a twelve-hour period in the order of their original projected arrival times, then the listener need not focus too hard until the projected time of their flight approaches. When doing this kind of listening, students may hit upon problems of this type: once, I had a class listen for the weather in a place they were supposedly going camping. However, they only knew the name of the national park, but did not know the name of the geographical area, and therefore failed to recognize "in the prairies" as telling them about their area of interest. An even more tricky problem arose when I had students listen for the time of a particular flight, and the message began, "All our flights are on time with the following exceptions . . ." and then went on only to list late flights. The flight we were listening for was not listed. This, in fact, turned the "listening for one specific detail" activity into a very sophisticated inferencing activity. Students had to go through the mental process of understanding the meaning of "with the following exceptions," listening to the whole message and using "rejecting strategies," determining that the flight they were interested in was not listed, and then making the inference that this meant that their flight was on time.

9.4. Listening for All the Details

This, too is "precision listening." Second-language listeners often approach all listening as if they always need to listen for all the details. This misconception is a function of their insecurity and, sadly, on occasion, also a result of the impression given by the ESL teacher and/or the ESL listening materials and tasks.

In fact, it is only necessary to listen for all the details in very specific situations. For example, if one is receiving directions how to get to a place, or how to do something step-by-step, then all the details, in the correct order, are essential. Similarly, if one is seeking professional advice, for example from a doctor, then it is advisable to get all the details. Another situation that calls for this skill is comparison shopping. When buying, say, a washing machine, it requires very careful listening in order to even grasp what the differences are between the different machines, other than price and capacity.

Listening for all the details will invariably call for note-taking (or list-making). There are very few situations in which it is necessary to get every detail, in which native speakers would trust their memory without the help of notes.

There are many different activities that can be developed for this type of listening. Some of the most enjoyable ones are those in which the learners' task does not end with getting down the salient points, but goes on to require that they *use* or *act upon* what they have heard. For example, they may be required to assemble something based on the listening plus note-taking. This follows the same principle of utilizing and applying academic notes, described in Section 9.2.

I have also found that students can be trained to listen for all the details in "comparison shopping" type situations by initially preparing skeleton charts for them, and later having them make notes freely. This would be an example in which they could, quite legitimately, be asked very precise questions of details on what they had been listening to.

9.5. Listening for Relaxation and Pleasure

It has long been recognized that we should not read all things in the same way, and that one of the most obvious distinctions is between reading for academic purposes and reading for pleasure. The same clearly holds for listening, but is not always reflected in listening courses. Second-language learners must be weaned away from the idea that every word and every detail is vital in everything that we listen to. There are many situations in which we listen, either to the radio or on video or at a movie, or to the lyrics of songs, strictly for pleasure. This does not mean that we should not concentrate, but it does affect the intensity with which we try to comprehend.

Clearly, the details are seldom important, and native speakers are seldom quizzed or called to account after listening for pleasure.

As ESL teachers, it is our responsibility to encourage our students to listen for relaxation and pleasure because this will motivate them to listen more which, in turn, will improve their English. It is therefore advisable to provide precisely such opportunities from time to time in the listening course, but then we must ensure that we do not "destroy" this by then asking all sorts of inappropriate questions—at most, they should be very general "impression" type questions.

9.6. Listening for the Gist

Linked very closely with the level of intensity with which we listen for pleasure is the type of listening that I call "listening for the gist." This is a type of listening that we do, for example, when coming in on the middle of a conversation, or when we switch on the radio or television not at a carefully planned time to listen to a specific program. This kind of listening justifies only the very broadest of questions such as, "What is this about?" (i.e., *What is the gist?*) It requires of listeners to use a number of the strategies described in earlier chapters, particularly those to determine topic. This kind of listening does not require a level of attention that would enable listeners to answer detailed questions, nor would it normally be accompanied by note-taking. It is the kind of listening that I typically do in the car in the mornings—the radio is always on, tuned to a morning talk show, and the talk tends to "wash over" me. At times, if a topic really interests me, I intensify my listening, but very often, by the time I reach my destination, all that I can remember of what I was listening to is the broad topic, say, pollution or the Olympics.

One of the features that distinguishes this kind of listening is that we go into it in the clear knowledge that we will *not* be questioned on it, nor, in fact, will we even be required to respond to it. All that we are after is the main idea. It is for this reason that I see "overhearing" or "eavesdropping" as being of this type. This must be distinguished from the listening we do for interactional purposes (see Section 9.9), because when eavesdropping, we are totally outside of the conversation.

9.7. Listening for Mood and Atmosphere

This type of listening is seldom done alone. However, it is important, and can on occasion be the main purpose of some listening. It is something that we need to do in the "eavesdropping" or "coming-in-on-the-middle-of-a-conversation" situations in particular. Clearly, the strategies advocated in the previous chapters would be activated, and listeners would be noticing what is being said, how it is being said, and the effect that this is having on the participants in the conversation. The strategies that are particularly helpful are those that were discussed in Section 6.4 on determining mood and atmosphere.

9.8. Listening on the Telephone

It might seem odd to have listed "listening on the telephone" as one of the main types of listening, when this might seem not to fit with the other types of listening, and, what is more, it can be argued that all sorts of listening goes on during telephone conversations. Listening on the telephone is, however, a special subset of interactive listening, and my overwhelming impression from talking to second-language learners for many years about listening is that they have a great deal of difficulty with it. In fact, it is very common for learners to be so intimidated by the telephone that they hesitate to use it. The reasons for the difficulty are clear: the sound quality is distorted and the visual signals that can be used in face-to-face communication are not there to be drawn on.

I would therefore advocate that a unit be devoted to listening to different things over the telephone, precisely to build up the students' confidence. I would concentrate on training them to cope with social "chat" in particular, since that is one of the most common uses of the telephone, and it is much of the affective signaling that they have to learn to do without.

9.9. Listening for Interactional Purposes

As was defined above, this is listening where the main purpose is not to glean specific information, or even the gist. It is more social intercourse—"chatting" and making small talk. A discussion of this kind of listening belongs more in a speaking course, as the main skills that learners need are to be able to sustain such conversation, to be a good "attender," and to use all the appropriate sociolinguistic signals so as to keep the channel of communication open, and to ensure good feeling between interlocutors. The need to *comprehend* as I have been using the term throughout this book is subordinate to these other factors.

9.10. Concluding Comments

A listening comprehension course cannot and should not be all things to all people. It is essential that the teacher and course designer be aware of the differences that exist between various types of listening discussed in this chapter and make their students aware of these differences, concentrating on those aspects that their students need.

10

Listening "for Real"

10.1. Introductory Comments

The very basis of a strategy-based approach to teaching listening comprehension is that the teacher's mandate is to teach students *how to tackle a listening passage* when not everything is comprehensible. And the teaching "how to" is through training in the use of different strategies. However, there comes a point at which everything has to be brought together, and learners have to be given practice in more lifelike listening, as opposed to the training activities that I have been advocating for different purposes. This requires that the tasks they are given are no longer cut up into little chunks, each training them to focus on some specific aspect or feature, nor is the material in any way "predigested" for them. What listeners should now be asked to do is appropriate, real tasks based on real listening material. This is as important a part of the listening comprehension course as the training activities, and care must be taken that any listening course provides learners with a large amount of such lifelike practice.

10.2. Listening Seldom Occurs Alone

As I have pointed out throughout this book, in reality, listening seldom occurs alone, and separating it out as I have done, has been for purposes of training students how to listen.

Throughout, I have acknowledged the artificiality of some of the training activities, and ultimately it is necessary to integrate listening with the other skills.[20]

---

[20] See also Pica (1984); Celce-Murcia (1987); Gilbert (1987); Murphy (1991).

When bringing everything together, some of the listening should be while participating in a conversation, and this requires that interlocutors jump from speaking to listening and back to speaking over and over in a very short space of time. Practice in this is usually found as part of a speaking course rather than as part of a listening course. I believe that it should also be provided in the latter part of a listening course, and special attention should be taken as to whether the speakers' responses are indeed responses to what has been said (how well they have been "attending"), and to what extent they are not real responses, but rather prepared utterances, prepared while the interlocutor was speaking.

A different kind of skills-integration is called for in academic listening (which invariably includes note-taking), which is intended to be synthesized with reading on the topic. Ultimately, students are usually expected to be able to do some sort of writing or speaking task based on the listening. An academic listening comprehension course must include working toward these integrated tasks. Teachers should try to replicate what students in academic courses really do with the listening. For example, they could listen to a lecture and then be given some reading on that topic, and the final task would be an oral or written presentation on the broader topic covered by both. An alternative task that I have given students is to do a "library research" project after listening to a lecture, in which they were required to find suitable material in the library (this skill plus library orientation would have been covered in the course), and synthesize or compare and contrast this with the information in the lecture. Clearly, this is only possible with fairly advanced students, but it certainly is much more meaningful and valuable to them than, for example, being "judged" merely on the quality of the notes that they took!

10.3. The "Jigsaw": An Example of an Activity that Pulls Everything Together

In jigsaw activities a task or question or problem is posed. Different students or groups of students are provided access to different aspects or parts of the solution (in our case through listening). The task can only be completed by learners trying to comprehend and interpret what they hear, and then pooling what they have gleaned in a collective attempt to resolve the question. This calls for listening of different types, and a fairly sophisticated level of predicting and inferencing. What is more, it calls for the integration of listening (probably with note-taking) and speaking, and can easily be developed to include reading and writing. Jigsaw activities can be used from an intermediate level upward, and the principle can be easily adapted for integrated academic tasks. Gillian Brown (1990:171–172) provides a good example of a jigsaw listening activity, and a textbook of such activities that I would highly recommend is Geddes and Sturtridge (1979).

10.4. Learner Autonomy

Learner autonomy is a major goal of a second-language listening comprehension course. I have argued that "strategies lead to autonomy." A strategy-based approach should not be seen as an end in itself, but as *a means to an end*, and that end is learner autonomy! In other words, what we should be striving for is a situation in which learners no longer need the teachers—we give them the training and hope they will be able to manage on their own even when we are not present. The analogy that comes to my mind is teaching children to ride a bicycle: we run alongside them, show them how to do it in stages, encourage them, hold the bicycle erect, etc., but eventually we let go, and they are able to ride without us!

It is not easy for teachers to let go and to acknowledge in their heart of hearts that making it possible for our students to manage without us is what we really are striving for. However, this is what we must aim for with most education, particularly adult education, and it certainly holds true for the approach that I have been advocating for listening comprehension. Ohliger (1975:39), writing about adult education in general, captures this idea poignantly:

> We are . . . caught in the near tragic grip of the spiraling dilemma that the more we contribute, in the name of "helping people," to the trend toward centralized control over people's lives . . . the less we can live the best ethics of our profession. Certainly one of these ethics is that adult educators work in partnership with individuals and groups to help them increase their responsible control over their lives.

10.5. Concluding Comments

I have argued that our goal and responsibility as teachers of listening comprehension to second-language learners is to teach learners how to listen. As Dunkel (1991) points out, this responsibility is increasing as we become "a world of listeners." Helping learners to listen is best achieved by training them to use a variety of strategies that will enable them to cope with the spoken language. The role, then, of the teacher is to be a strategy trainer—to train learners to use and apply the strategies that will make them good and self-sufficient listeners.

References

Alderson, J. C. and A. H. Urquhart 1985. "This Test is Unfair. I'm not an Economist." In Hauptman, LeBlanc, and Wesche, eds., 25–43.

Allwright, R. L. 1980. "What do We Want Teaching Materials for?" Paper presented at TESOL International Conference, San Francisco.

Anderson, A. and T. Lynch 1988. Listening. Oxford: Oxford University Press.

Anderson, R. C., J. Osborn, and R. J. Tierney, eds. 1984. Learning to Read in American Schools: Basal Readers and Content Texts. New Jersey: Erlbaum.

Anderson, R. C., R. E. Reynolds, D. L. Schallert, and E. T. Goetz 1977. "Frameworks for Comprehending Discourse." American Educational Research Journal 14, 4:367–381.

Anderson, T. H. and B. B. Armbruster 1984. "Content Area Textbooks." In Anderson, Osborn, and Tierney, eds., 193–226.

Asher, J. 1969. "The Total Physical Response Approach to Second Language Learning." Modern Language Journal 53:3–17.

Avery, P. and S. Ehrlich, eds. 1992. Teaching American English Pronunciation. Oxford: Oxford University Press.

Bartlett, F. C. 1932. Remembering: A Study in Experimental and Social Psychology. Cambridge: Cambridge University Press.

Beebe, L. 1985. "Input: Choosing the Right Stuff." In Gass and Madden, eds., 404–414.

Benson, J. D., W. S. Greaves, and D. J. Mendelsohn 1988. "The Centrality of Intonation in English: An Experimental Validation of Some Aspects of M. A. K. Halliday's Theory of Intonation in a Canadian Context." In Fawcett and Young, eds., 39–51.

Benson, M. J. 1989. "The Academic Listening Task." TESOL Quarterly 23, 3:421–447.

Blau, E. K. 1990. "The Effect of Syntax, Speed, and Pauses on Listening Comprehension." TESOL Quarterly 24, 4:746–753.

Brown, A. L. and A. S. Palincsar 1982. "Inducing Strategic Learning from Texts by means of Informed, Self-control Training." Topics in Learning and Learning Disabilities 2, 1:1–17.

Brown, George, and M. Bakhtar 1983. Styles of Lecturing. Report, University of Nottingham.

Brown, Gillian 1977. Listening to Spoken English, First Edition. London: Longman.

Brown, Gillian 1978. "Understanding Spoken English." TESOL Quarterly 12, 3:271–283.

Brown, Gillian 1987. "Twenty Five Years of Teaching Listening Comprehension." English Teaching Forum 25, 4:11–15.

Brown, Gillian 1990. Listening to Spoken English, Second Edition. London: Longman.

Brown, Gillian, and George Yule 1983. Teaching the Spoken Language. Cambridge: Cambridge University Press.

Brown, H. D. 1989. A Practical Guide to Language Learning: A Fifteen-Week Program of Strategies for Success. New York: McGraw Hill.

Brown, H. D. 1991. Breaking the Language Barrier. Yarmouth, ME: Intercultural Press.

Burbridge, B. 1986. "Looking at Volcanoes and Listening Comprehension." TESOL Newsletter 20, 4:7–11.

Byrnes, H. 1984. "The Role of Listening Comprehension: A Theoretical Base." Foreign Language Annals 17, 4:317–329.

Caffrey, J. 1955. "Auding Ability at the Secondary Level." Education 75:303–310.

Campione, J. C., and B. Armbruster 1985. "Acquiring Information from Texts: An Analysis of Four Approaches." In Segal, Chipman, and Glaser, eds., 317–359.

Canale, M. and M. Swain 1980. "Theoretical Bases of Communicative Approaches to Second Language Teaching and Testing." Applied Linguistics 1, 1:1–47.

Carrell, P. L. 1984. "Evidence of a Formal Schema in Second Language Comprehension." Language Learning 34, 2:87–112.

Carrell, P. L., and J. C. Eisterhold 1983. "Schema Theory and ESL Reading Pedagogy." TESOL Quarterly 17, 4:553–573.

Carton, A. 1966. The Method of Inference in Foreign Language Study. New York: The Research Foundation of the City of New York.

Carver, D. 1984. "Plans, Learner Strategies and Self Direction in Language Learning." System 12, 2:123–131.

Celce-Murcia, M. 1987. "Teaching Pronunciation as Communication." In Morley, ed., 1–12.

Celce-Murcia, M., ed. 1991. Teaching English as a Second or Foreign Language, Second Edition. Boston: Heinle and Heinle.

Chamot, A. U. 1987. "The Learning Strategies of ESL Students." In Wenden and Rubin, eds., 71–83.

Chamot, A. U., and L. Kupper 1989. "Learning Strategies in Foreign Language Instruction." Foreign Language Annals 22, 1:13–24.

Chamot, A. U., and J. M. O'Malley 1987. "The Cognitive Academic Language Learning Approach: A Bridge to the Mainstream." TESOL Quarterly 21, 2:227–250.

Chaudron, C., J. Cook, and L. Loschky 1988. "Quality of Lecture Notes and Second Language Listening Comprehension." University of Hawaii: Technical Report No. 5, Center for Second Language Classroom Research.

Chaudron, C., and J. C. Richards 1986. "The Effect of Discourse Markers on the Comprehension of Lectures." Applied Linguistics 7:113–127.

Chiang, C. S., and P. Dunkel 1992. "The Effect of Speech Modification, Prior Knowledge and Listening Proficiency on EFL Lecture Learning." TESOL Quarterly 26, 2:345–374.

Clark, H., and E. Clark 1977. Psychology and Language. New York: Harcourt Brace Jovanovich.

Clarke, M. A. 1980. "The Short Circuit Hypothesis of ESL Reading—or When Language Competence Interferes with Reading Performance. Modern Language Journal 64:203–209.

Clarke, M. A., and S. Silberstein 1977. "Toward a Realization of Psycholinguistic Principles in the ESL Reading Class." Language Learning 27, 1:135–154.

Cohen, A. D. 1990. Language Learning: Insights for Learners, Teachers and Researchers. New York: Newbury House.

Cohen, A. D. 1991. "Strategies in Second Language Learning: Insights from Research." In Phillipson, Kellerman, Selinker, Sharwood Smith, and Swain, eds., 107–119.

Cohen, A. D. 1992. "The Teacher's Role in Learner Strategy Training: An Innovation in Teacher Education." In Flowerdew, Brock, and Hsia, eds., 241–252.

Cohen, A. D., and C. Hosenfeld 1981. "Some Uses of Mentalistic Data in Second Language Research." Language Learning 31:285–314.

Crookall, D. 1983. "Learner Training: A Neglected Strategy. Part 1 and Part 2." Modern English Teacher 11, 1:31–33 (Part 1), 11, 2:41–42 (Part 2).

Derry, S. J., and D. A. Murphy 1986. "Designing Systems that Train Learning Ability: From Theory to Practice." Review of Educational Research 56:1–39.

Dudley-Evans, A., and T. F. Johns 1981. "A Team Approach to Lecture Comprehension for Overseas Students." The Teaching of Listening Comprehension.

Dunkel, P. 1985. "Listening and Note-Taking: What is the Effect of Pre-Training in Note-Taking?" TESOL Newsletter 19:30–31.

Dunkel, P. 1986. "Developing Listening Fluency in L2: Theoretical Principles and Pedagogical Considerations." Modern Language Journal 70, 2:99–106.

Dunkel, P. 1991. "Listening in the Native and Second/Foreign Language: Toward an Integration of Research and Practice." TESOL Quarterly 25, 3:431 458.

Ekman, P., and W. Friesen 1969. "The Repertoire of Non-Verbal Behavior: Categories, Origins, Usage and Coding." Semiotica 1:49–98.

Ellis, G., and B. Sinclair 1989a. Learning to Learn English: A Course in Learner Training, Learner's Book. Cambridge: Cambridge University Press.

Ellis, G., and B. Sinclair 1989b. Learning to Learn English: A Course in Learner Training, Teacher's Book. Cambridge: Cambridge University Press.

Fawcett, R., and D. Young, eds. 1988. New Developments in Systemic Linguistics. Volume 2: Theory and Application. London: Pinter Publications.

Faerch, C., and G. Kasper 1986. "The Role of Comprehension in Second Language Learning." Applied Linguistics 7:257–274.

Flowerdew, J., M. Brock, and S. Hsia, eds. 1992. Perspectives on Second Language Teacher Education. Kowloon: City Polytechnic of Hong Kong.

Floyd, P., and P. Carrell 1987. "Effects on ESL Reading of Teaching Cultural Content Schemata." Language Learning 37:89–108.

Frawley, W., ed. 1982. Linguistics and Literacy. New York: Plenum Press.

Gardner, R. C., and P. C. Smythe 1975. Language Research Group National Test Battery, Form A. London: University of Western Ontario.

Gass, S. 1983. "The Development of L2 Intuitions." TESOL Quarterly 17:273–291.

Gass, S., and C. Madden, eds. 1985. Input in Second Language Acquisition. Rowley, MA: Newbury House.

Geddes, M. 1988. How to Listen. London: British Broadcasting Corporation.

Geddes, M., and G. Sturtridge 1979. Listening Links. London: Heinemann.

Gilbert, J. B. 1984. Clear Speech. First Edition. New York: Cambridge University Press.

Gilbert, J. B. 1987. "Pronunciation and Listening Comprehension." In Morley, ed., 2940.

Gilbert, J. B. 1993. Clear Speech. Second Edition. New York: Cambridge University Press.

Glisan, E.W. 1988. "A Plan for Teaching Listening Comprehension: Adaptation of an Instructional Reading Model." Foreign Language Annals 21, 1:9–16.

Gregory, M. 1967. "Aspects of Varieties Differentiation." Journal of Linguistics 3, 2:177–198.

Griffin, V. 1981. "Self-directed Adult Learners and Learning." In Herman, ed., 21–39.

Halliday, M. A. K. 1967. Intonation and Grammar in British English. The Hague: Mouton.

Halliday, M. A. K., and R. Hasan 1976. Cohesion in English. London: Longman.

Hamp-Lyons, L. 1983. "Review of: Survey of Materials for Teaching Advanced Listening and Note-Taking." TESOL Quarterly 17, 1:109–121.

Hauptman P., R. LeBlanc, and M. Wesche, eds. 1985. Second Language Performance Testing. Ottawa: University of Ottawa Press.

Henner-Stanchina, C. 1982. "Listening Comprehension Strategies and Autonomy: Why Error Analysis?" Melanges Pedagogiques, 53–64.

Herman, R., ed. 1981. The Design of Self-Directed Learning. Toronto: OISE, Adult Education Department.

Higgs, T. V., ed. 1984. Teaching for Proficiency, the Organizing Principle. Lincolnwood, IL: National Textbook.

Hinde, R. A., ed. 1972. Non-Verbal Communication. Cambridge: Cambridge University Press.

Holec, H. 1981. Autonomy and Foreign Language Learning. Oxford: Pergamon.

Holec, H. 1985. "On Autonomy: Some Elementary Concepts." In Riley, ed., 173–190.

Hollow, M.K. 1955. "Listening Comprehension at the Intermediate Grade Level." Elementary School Journal 56:156–161.

Hosenfeld, C. 1976. "Learning about Learning: Discovering Our Students' Strategies." Foreign Language Annals 9:117–129.

Hosenfeld, C. 1979. "A Learning-Teaching View of Second Language Instruction." Foreign Language Annals 12:41–54.

Johnson, P. 1981. "Effects on Reading Comprehension of Language Complexity and Cultural Background of a Text." TESOL Quarterly 15:169–181.

Johnstone, J. W. C. 1963. "The Educational Pursuits of American Adults." Adult Education 13:217–222.

Joiner, E. G. 1991. "Teaching Listening: Ends and Means." In Linguistics and Language Pedagogy: The State of the Art, 1–19.

Jones, B.F., A.S. Palincsar, D.S. Ogle, and G. Carr, eds. 1987. Strategic Teaching and Learning: Cognitive Instruction in the Content Areas. Alexandria, VA: Association for Supervision and Curriculum Development in Co-operation with the North Central Region Educational Laboratory.

Keefe, J. W. 1979. "Learning Style: An Overview." In Keefe, ed., 1–17.

Keefe, J. W., ed. 1979. Student Learning Styles: Diagnosing and Prescribing Programs. Reston, VA: National Association of Secondary School Principals.

Kellerman, S. 1992a. "Survey Review: Recent Materials for the Teaching of Listening." ELT Journal 46, 1:100–112.

Kellerman, S. 1992b. " 'I See what you Mean.' The Role of Kinesic Behaviour in Listening and Implications for Foreign and Second Language Learning." Applied Linguistics 13, 3:239–258.

Kidd, J. R. 1973. How Adults Learn. New York: Association Press.

Knowles, M. 1970. The Modern Practice of Adult Education. New York: Association Press.

Krashen, S. D. 1983. "Bilingual Education and Second Language Acquisition Theory." In Schooling and Language Minority Students: A Theoretical Framework, 51–79.

Krashen, S., and T. Terrell 1983. The Natural Approach: Language Acquisition in the Classroom. Oxford: Pergamon Press.

Kress, G. 1990. "Critical Discourse Analysis." Annual Review of Applied Linguistics 11:84–99.

Langer, J. A. 1981. "From Theory to Practice: A Pre-Reading Plan." Journal of Reading 25:152–156.

Lee, J. F. 1986. "Background Knowledge and L2 Reading." Modern Language Journal 70:350–354.

Linguistics and Language Pedagogy: The State of the Art 1991. Georgetown: Georgetown University Round Table on Languages and Linguistics.

Long, D. R. 1989. "Second Language Listening Comprehension: A Schema-Theoretic Perspective." Modern Language Journal 73:32–40.

Lougheed, L. 1985. Listening between the Lines: A Cultural Approach. Reading, MA: Addison-Wesley.

Lund, R. 1990. "A Taxonomy for Teaching Second Language Listening." Foreign Language Annals 23:105–115.

Lyons, J. 1972. "Human Language." In R.A. Hinde, ed., 49–85.

McClelland, J. L., D. E. Rumelhart, and the PDP Research Group, eds. 1986. Parallel Distributed Processing: Explorations in the Microstructure of Cognition. Volume 2: Psychological and Biological Models. Cambridge, MA: MIT Press (A Bradford Book).

McClendon, P. I. 1957. "An Experimental Study of the Relationship between the Note-Taking Practices and Listening Comprehension of College Freshmen During Expository Lectures." Speech Monographs 24:95–96.

McGroarty, M. 1987. "Patterns of Persistent Second Language Learners: Elementary Spanish." Paper presented at TESOL International Conference, Miami.

McNerney, M. and D. Mendelsohn 1992. "Suprasegmentals in the Pronunciation Class: Setting Priorities." In Avery and Ehrlich, eds., 185–196.

Mendelsohn, D. 1984. "There ARE Strategies for Listening." TEAL Occasional Papers 8:63–76.

Mendelsohn, D. 1992. "A Strategy-Based Approach to the Teaching of Listening Comprehension." Plenary Address presented at TESOL International Conference, Vancouver.

Morley, J., ed. 1987. Current Perspectives on Pronunciation. Washington: TESOL.

Morley, J. 1991. "Listening Comprehension in Second/Foreign Language Instruction." In Celce-Murcia, ed., 81–106.

Moulden, H. 1985. "Extending Self-Directed Learning of English in an Engineering College." In Riley, ed., 206–232.

Mueller, G. A. 1980. "Visual Contextual Cues and Listening Comprehension: An Experiment." Modern Language Journal 64:335–340.

Murphy, J. M. 1985. "Examining ESL Listening as an Interpretive Process." TESOL Newsletter XIX, 6:23–24.

Murphy, J. M. 1987. "The Listening Strategies of English as a Second Language College Students." Research and Teaching in Developmental Education 4, 1:27–46.

Murphy, J. M. 1991. "Oral Communication in TESOL: Integrating Speaking, Listening and Pronunciation." TESOL Quarterly 25, 1:51–76.

Naiman, N., M. Frohlich, H. H. Stern, and A. Todesco 1978. "The Good Language Learner." Research in Education 7, Toronto: OISE.

Nichols, R. G. 1955. "Ten Components of Effective Listening." Education 75, 5:292–302.

Noller, P. 1984. Nonverbal Communication and Marital Interaction. Oxford: Pergamon Press.

Nord, J. 1980. "Developing Listening Fluency before Speaking." System 8:1–22.

Nunan, D. 1988. Designing Communicative Tasks for the Language Classroom. Cambridge: Cambridge University Press.

Ohliger, J. 1975. "Prospects for a Learning Society." Adult Leadership Sept., 37–39.

Omaggio, A. 1978. "Successful Language Learners: What do We Know about Them?" ERIC/CLL News Bulletin May.

Omaggio-Hadley, A. 1993. Teaching Language in Context. Second Edition. Boston: Heinle and Heinle.

O'Malley, J. M. 1987. "The Effects of Training in the Use of Learning Strategies on Acquiring English as a Second Language." In Wenden and Rubin, eds., 133–144.

O'Malley, J. M., and A. U. Chamot 1990. Learning Strategies in Second Language Acquisition. Cambridge: Cambridge University Press.

O'Malley, J. M., A. U. Chamot, and L. Kupper 1989. "Listening Comprehension Strategies in Second Language Acquisition." Applied Linguistics 10, 4:418–435.

O'Malley, J. M., A. U. Chamot, G. Stewner-Manzanares, L. Kupper, and R.P. Russo 1985. "Learning Strategies Used by Beginning and Intermediate ESL Students." Language Learning 35, 1:21–46.

Oxford, R. 1987. "Lessons from Research on Language Learning Strategies." Unpublished Manuscript.

Oxford, R. (1990). Language Learning Strategies: What Every Teacher Should Know. New York: Newbury House.

Oxford, R. 1993. "Research Update on Teaching L2 Listening." System 21, 2:205–211.

Oxford, R., R. Z. Lavine, and D. Crookall 1989. "Language Learning Strategies, the Communicative Approach, and their Classroom Implications." Foreign Language Annals 22, 1:29–39.

Peterson, P. W. 1991. "A Synthesis of Models for Interactive Listening." In Celce-Murcia, ed., 106–122.

Phillipson, R., E. Kellerman, L. Selinker, M. Sharwood Smith, and M. Swain, eds. 1991. Foreign/Second Language Pedagogy Research: A Commemorative Volume for Claus Faerch. Clevedon, U.K.: Multilingual Matters.

Pica, T. 1984. "Pronunciation Activities with an Accent on Communication". English Teaching Forum 22, 3:2–6.

Porte, G. 1988. "Poor Language Learners and their Strategies for Dealing with New Vocabulary." English Language Teaching Journal 42, 3:167–172.

Porter, D., and J. Roberts 1981. "Authentic Listening Activities." English Language Teaching Journal 36:37–47.

Prabhu, N.S. 1987. Second Language Pedagogy: A Perspective. Oxford: Oxford University Press.

Prowse, R. 1983. "Talking about Learning." TESOL France News 3, 2:18–19.

Reid, J. 1987. "The Learning Style Preferences of ESL Students." TESOL Quarterly 21, 1:87–112.

Richards, J. C. 1983. "Listening Comprehension: Approach, Design, Procedure." TESOL Quarterly 17, 2:219–240.

Richards, J. C. 1990. The Language Teaching Matrix. Cambridge: Cambridge University Press.

Riley, P. 1982. "Topics in Communicative Methodology: Including a Preliminary and Selective Bibliography on the Communicative Approach." Melanges Pedagogiques. 93–132.

Riley, P., ed. 1985. Discourse and Learning. London: Longman.

Rivers, W. M. 1981. Teaching Foreign Language Skills. Second Edition. Chicago: University of Chicago Press.

Rost, M. 1990. Listening in Language Learning. London: Longman.

Rost, M. 1991. Listening in Action: Activities for Developing Listening in Language Teaching. New York: Prentice Hall.

Rost, M., and S. Ross 1991. "Learner Use of Strategies in Interaction: Typology and Teachability." Language Learning 41, 2:235–273.

Rubin, J. 1975. "What the 'Good Language Learner' Can Teach Us." TESOL Quarterly 9, 1:41–50.

Rubin, J. 1981. "Study of Cognitive Processes in Second Language Learning." Applied Linguistics 11, 2:117–131.

Rubin, J. 1987. "Learner Strategies: Theoretical Assumptions, Research History and Typology." In Wenden and Rubin, eds., 15– 30.

Rubin, J. 1988. "Improving Foreign Language Listening Comprehension." Research Report on Project #017AH70028 Sept. Washington, DC: U.S. Dept. of Education, International Research and Studies Program.

Ruetten, M. K. 1986. Comprehending Academic Lectures. New York: Maxwell Macmillan.

Rumelhart, D. E. 1980. "Schemata: The Building Blocks of Cognition." In Spiro, Bruce, and Brewer, eds., 33–58.

Rumelhart, D. E., P. Smolensky, J. L. McClelland, and G. E. Hinton 1986. "Schemata and Sequential Thought Processes in PDP Models." In McClelland, Rumelhart, and the PDP Research Group, eds., 7–57.

Schank, R. C., and R. P. Abelson 1977. Scripts, Plans, Goals and Understanding. Hillsdale, NJ: Erlbaum.

Schmeck, R. R. 1981. "Improving Learning by Improving Thinking." Educational Leadership 38:384–385.

Schooling and language Minority Students: A Theoretical Framework 1983. Sacramento: California State Department of Education, Office of Bilingual Bicultural Education.

Segal, J. W., S. F. Chipman, and R. Glaser, eds. 1985. Thinking and Learning Skills. Volume 1. Hillsdale, NJ: Erlbaum.

Sharwood Smith, M. 1981. "Consciousness-Raising and the Second Language Learner." Applied Linguistics 2, 2:159–168.

Snow, B. G., and K. Perkins 1979. "The Teaching of Listening Comprehension and Communication Activities." TESOL Quarterly 13, 1:51–63.

Spearrit, D. 1962. "Listening Comprehension—a Factorial Analysis." Australian Council for Educational Research Series 76.

Sperber, D., and D. Wilson 1986. Relevance. Oxford: Basil Blackwell.

Spiro, R. J., B. C. Bruce, and W. F. Brewer, eds. 1980. Theoretical Issues in Reading Comprehension. Hillsdale, NJ: Erlbaum.

Steffensen, M. S., C. Joag-dev, and R. C. Anderson 1979. "A Cross-Cultural Perspective on Reading Comprehension. Reading Research Quarterly 15:10–29.

Stern, H. H. 1975. "What we can Learn from the Good Language Learner." Canadian Modern Language Review 31:304–318.

Stevens, K. 1982. "Can we Improve Reading by Teaching Background Information?" Journal of Reading 25:326–329.

Stevick, E. W. 1984. "Curriculum Development at the Foreign Service Institute." In Higgs, ed., 85–112.

Stevick, E. W. 1989. Success with Foreign Languages: Seven Who Achieved It and What Worked for Them. Englewood Cliffs: Prentice-Hall.

Stewner-Manzanares, G., A. U. Chamot, J. M. O'Malley, L. Kupper, and R. P. Russo 1983. A Teacher's Guide for Using Learning Strategies in Acquiring ESL. Rosslyn, VA: Inter-America Research Associates.

Tannen, D. 1982. "The Myth of Orality and Literacy." In Frawley, ed., 37–50.

Twaddell, F. 1973. "Vocabulary Expansion in the ESOL Classroom." TESOL Quarterly 7, 1:61–78.

Tyacke, M., and D. Mendelsohn 1986. "Student Needs: Cognitive as well as Communicative." TESL Canada Journal Special Issue No. 1:171–183.

Underwood, M. 1989. Teaching Listening. London: Longman.

Ur, P. 1984. Teaching Listening Comprehension. Cambridge: Cambridge University Press.

Vann, R. A, and R. G. Abraham 1990. "Strategies of Unsuccessful Language Learners." TESOL Quarterly 20, 2:177–198.

Verner, C., and G. Dickinson 1967. "The Lecture: An Analysis and Review of Research." Adult Education 17:85–00.

Weissenreider, M. 1987. "Listening to the News in Spanish." Modern Language Journal 71:18–27.

Wenden, A. 1983. "Literature Review: The Process of Intervention." Language Learning 33, 1:103–121.

Wenden, A. 1985. "Learner Strategies." TESOL Newsletter XIX, 5:1–7.

Wenden, A. 1987. "Incorporating Learner Training in the Classroom." In Wenden and Rubin, eds., 159–168.

Wenden, A. 1988. "Learner Strategies for Learner Autonomy: Planning and Implementing Learner Training for L2 Learners." Unpublished manuscript. New York.

Wenden, A., A. U. Chamot, A. D. Cohen, D. Mendelsohn, M. Nyikos, J. M. O'Malley, R. Oxford, J. Rubin, and M. Tyacke 1989. "Promoting L2 Learner Autonomy through Learning Strategy Applications." Colloquium presented at TESOL International Conference, San Antonio.

Wenden, A., and J. Rubin, eds. 1987. Learning Strategies in Language Learning. Englewood Cliffs: Prentice-Hall.

Willing, K. 1987. "Learning Strategies as Information Management." Prospect 2, 3:273–291.

Willing, K. 1988a. Learning Styles in Adult Migrant Education. Australia: National Curriculum Resource Centre: Adult Migrant Education Program.

Willing, K. 1988b. "Learning Strategies as Information Management: Some Definitions for a Theory of Learning Strategies." Prospect 3, 2:139–156.

Willing, K. 1989. Teaching How to Learn: Learning Strategies in ESL. Activity Worksheets and Teachers Guide. Sydney: National Centre for English Language Teaching and Research, Macquarie University.

Yorio, C. 1982. "The Language Learner: A Consumer with Opinions." Paper presented at TESOL International Conference, Hawaii.

Young, L., and B. Fitzgerald 1982. Listening and Learning. Rowley, MA: Newbury House.

Yuan, D-z. 1982. "Chinese Scientists' Difficulties in Comprehending English Science Lectures." M.A. Thesis, Los Angeles: University of California at Los Angeles.